orientation

Other Books by the Author (selected)

Erotic Massage for Healing and Pleasure

Art and Survival: Patricia Johanson's Environmental Projects

Culturing Sustainability: A Cookbook for Artists and Educators

Edited by the Author (selected)

Give Back: First Nations Perspectives on Cultural Practice

Forbidden Subjects: Self-Portraits by Lesbian Artists

In My Country: An Anthology of Canadian Artists

orientation
mapping queer meanings

caffyn jesse

foreward by paula stromberg

erospirit

LIBRARY AND ARCHIVES CANADA CATALOGUING IN PUBLICATION

Jesse, Caffyn, author
    Orientation : mapping queer meanings / Caffyn Jesse.

Includes bibliographical references. ISBN 978-0-9738332-2-5 (paperback)
    1. Homosexuality. 2. Sexual orientation. 3. Homophobia. 4. Gays--Identity.
5. Stereotypes (Social psychology). 6. Archetypes in civilization. I. Title.

HQ76.25.J48 2015   306.76'6   C2015-906153-9

Cover and book design by Mark Hand

Illustrations on page 70 and 160 are courtesy of Age Photostock. Photos by Mehdi Naimi and Penny Robertshaw are published with permission of the photographers. Illustrations with no known copyright restrictions are gathered from Wikimedia Commons, the Wellcome library, and other sources.

Contents

An angel locking or unlocking the gates of Hell with a key, miniature from the Winchester Psalter, British Library, London. Circa 1121-1161, Wikimedia

Queering the Mainstream

Foreword by Paula Stromberg

Reviewing this extraordinary book about queer activism, I am struck by the unique perspectives it offers on the big public issues of our times — issues such as environmental concerns, climate change, and global economic justice.

At this time in history, there is an urgent need for finding new ways to exist on our planet. We need new approaches to our relationship with nature, food security, financial and economic systems, and better ways to address drastic income disparity.

Business as usual has to change. In this book, author, artist, and activist Caffyn Jesse describes how exploring queer difference can offer insights that challenge core structures in society, including gender oppressions, international conversation about our economic systems, and our approach to the ruling class of elites. These exciting ideas could energize the next wave of queer activism.

What if we worked to "queer the mainstream" instead of always trying to "mainstream the queers"?

Yes, queers in many countries around the world have won legal rights. In 2015 same-sex marriage is legally recognized in about twenty countries. Understanding and acceptance of trans people has never been greater in world history. Queers are harvesting their achieve-

7

ments. But I know from my own work with LGBTQ (Lesbian, Gay, Bisexual, Transgender and Queer) people in Africa, Asia and North America that we must not relax. While queer lives unfold so differently within each country, homophobic stereotypes have global currency. These stereotypes are used to fan the flames of hatred, generating violence, prejudice and death.

Jesse makes the radical suggestion that queer resistance can change these wounding stereotypes into empowering archetypes that help us think differently, more deeply, about our social function. In her explorations of the many homophobic stereotypes associated with queer difference, she demonstrates how using "the energy the enemy gives us" can shape new ways of living. As in the Aikido martial arts principle of turning an aggressor's energy back on itself — she suggests we enter the attack, move toward it, and transform it.

Jesse does see great value in the civil rights struggles that advocate for mainstreaming the queers. Because of these struggles, she says, "I feel safer in my community and my skin." Yet if queers seek only tolerance and integration, we settle for far less than we need and can imagine. Instead of fighting only for the right to equality within an unjust system, fighting only to be accepted as ordinary, fighting only for the right to subside into mainstream society, queers might simultaneously use their capacity for transgression to envision and implement radical alternatives.

Jesse has long encouraged the LGBTQ community not to simply seek acceptance, but to work towards a transformed culture in which queer difference is seen and celebrated. For the past few decades, she has brought this critical perspective to her work as a community activist, artist, editor, teacher, author, and somatic sex educator. "Queer people can use their understanding of oppression to challenge the ways oppression functions. We can claim a unique perspective on gender difference, and the culture of nature, race, sex and family," she says.

Her writing, artwork and activism on this subject go back to the 1980's. Much of the research in this volume was published online in 2004. The 2015 publication of *Orientation: Mapping Queer Meanings* gathers Jesse's thirty-five years of cultural innovation into a single, potent volume.

Orientation: Mapping Queer Meanings is also a meditation on avenues for exploring the soul's growth. Jesse says that queer difference can encourage us to redefine the scope of our souls. "With every image, pattern and archetype we build into the web of nature and society, we make ourselves and the world more queer, and so at once more fabulous, more complicated, and more whole."

Orientation is an intriguing, thought-provoking and spirit-expanding book by an important writer.

Paula Stromberg
Phnom Penh, Cambodia, November 2015

Paula Stromberg collaborates internationally with young activists on video documentaries, covering women's empowerment and human rights issues around the world. She has produced Family is Like Skin: Lesbians in Cambodia, Salary Hunger- Garment Workers in Cambodia, and other short movies.

The Kangjiashimenji Petroglyphs are bas-relief carvings from circa 1000 **BC**, in the Xinjiang region of northwest China. Some of the figures combine elements of male and female, they are ithyphallic but wear female headwear, a decoration on the chest, and sometimes a mask.
They are shown having sex with male and female figures.

Introduction

This year, the Pride Parade on Salt Spring Island was all joyous. There were so many community participants: little children, elders, farmers, middle school students, yoga teachers, a church, and many progressive community groups. People dressed in rainbow colours and donned sexually-exuberant, gender-bending costumes. We danced, sang and celebrated the special meanings and beauties of queer love, lives and identities. The parade was a high-spirited and happy occasion, marking the significant legal victories and social freedoms that people who identify as gay, lesbian, bisexual, transgender, gender-variant or queer (GLBTQ) have achieved over the past fifteen years.

The face of prejudice was different when I began working with the ideas in this book in workshops I presented from 1999 and a website published in 2004. Decades of queer activism have addressed civil rights issues and helped to "normalize" GLBTQ existence. The first Pride celebrations in my community in 2005 were tentative, and those involved in presenting them were fearful. Now – on Salt Spring Island at least – Pride celebrations are honoured as a significant tourist draw, sponsored by local businesses. Yet even in a place that is widely known as a "tolerant" community, there is significant resistance. Last year there was a rainbow flag burning and vandalism to parade route markers.

It is important to savour these safe zones and moments of relative freedom created through decades of activism. And it is also important to notice that many deep social issues remain unchanged. Homophobia remains embedded in everyday behaviours, language, and institutional policies. Homophobic stereotypes profoundly affect our lives, often in proportion to our precarity. Those who are poor, young, old or gender-nonconforming experience the most precarity. Queer youth are socially isolated and unsafe. Even on queer-friendly Salt Spring Island, high school students are clear that stereotypes regulating gender and sexual orientation have violent consequences, and maintain a chilling grip on all their lives.[1] Queer elders are often isolated, and live without predictability or security. Fear infects the lives and shapes the deaths of GLBTQ people. The unsafe environments created by homophobia structure the lives and identities of all who come of age in the cultures they characterize. This book discusses homophobia in particular, but it is important to note that transphobia operates through distinct though related cultural paradigms and stereotypes that damage and limit us.

How does homosexuality come to pose such a radical threat? Same-sex passions are everywhere and ordinary, throughout nature and around the world. Yet fearsome and terrible notions of who we are still seize the popular imagination, and find continual expression in popular culture. In cultural terms, homosexuality is evidently much more than the ordinary, enduring fact of same-sex sexual preference. Homophobia impresses each queer life with a bone-deep knowledge that our difference holds a terrible variety of meanings, a bewildering complex of allusions and associations. The Christian Right says, "The gay agenda is the devil's agenda."[2] Sexual lasciviousness, disease, treason, cowardice, the abuse of children, the contamination of blood – every imaginable evil is linked with homosexuality. Henning Bech comments, "there is no evil that the homosexual cannot embody."[3] We are accused of acting against god, family values, the national interest, and evolutionary logic. "We're talking about the deconstruction of American society," says Christian Coalition of Georgia Leader Sadie Fields.[4] The symbolic figure of "the homosexual" is a monster. And though this bogeyman is far removed from manifestly ordinary queer lives, we are forced to live with the consequences of its construction.

The strategy of the contemporary GLBTQ civil rights movement has been to counter homophobic stereotypes by asserting a profusion of counter-stereotypes. We protest our innocence, and claim that homosexuality is natural, ordinary and uninteresting. What would happen if, instead, we acknowledged our fearsomeness, and explored the power that homophobic stereotypes invest in homosexuality? Instead of always deflecting the blows that homophobia metes out, we could learn, as in Eastern martial arts, to "go with the blow." It is a way of using the energy the enemy gives us.

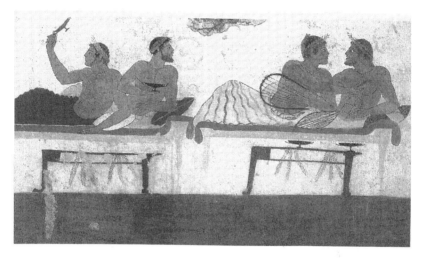

Tomb of the Diver, Paestum, 480 BC, Greek wall painting. Wikimedia.

We can ask what it means to acknowledge that homosexuality is associated with the end of the world as we know it – not to uncover meanings hidden inside us, but rather, as a kind of "tuning in" to the allusions and associations broadcast by the cultural phenomenon of homosexuality. To examine what homosexuality signifies, we can listen to the noise it makes. How does homosexuality resonate throughout the culture, in connection with other cultural constructs like gender, nature, family and race? What does this imply for those of us who aim and claim to "be" homosexual? This book explores these questions.

I find a kind of magic in those notions of homosexuality that can be described as homophobic stereotypes. Stereotypes are undistinguished, trite and obvious images that keep us locked in empty nothings. Archetypes are powerful, living symbols that link us to myth and history. Yet both can be described in the way Carl Jung speaks of archetypes: both stereotypes and archetypes are "involuntary manifestations of unconscious processes,"[5] or "the thoughts that think you." So often, stereotypes that oppress queer people open into archetypes. Vengeful witch, stone butch, effeminate man, pedophile, androgyne, wild man, clown – such figures have rich historical antecedents. They express aspects of human experience that claim symbolic presence in the myths and dreams of many cultures.

Contemporary Western culture has no great myths. It tells no stories of magic and transformation. But it talks ceaselessly of homosexuals. In a world that is contemptuous of sacrament and mystery, there is still one way to evoke a place of secrecy, depth, gigantic risk, erotic power, the quality of being "impossible." There is being queer. Instead of witches, warrior-women and virgin mothers, there are lesbians. Instead of fools, martyrs, water-spirits and vegetation gods, there are gay men. Homosexual people can be seen to represent the mythic narratives and potentialities of contemporary Western culture. The constructed identity of homosexuality could hold this journey inside it, as a blossom could hold an apple – not an essence, but a possibility – a whisper, a promise, a blueprint, an inner impulse. If we can seize hold of the rich variety of meanings that inhere in queer identities, we can assume these powers.

The archetypes, stereotypes and images in which we are enmeshed are an enormous burden. I see them also as a gigantic opportunity. The net of meanings that surrounds us as queer people links us with myth, history, and the capacity to transform society. In this book my point is not to interpret, nor even less to untangle, this web of association. I aim not to explain and dispose of stereotypes, but to amplify them. I approach the multi-layered meanings that accrue to homosexuality through reflection and poetry as well as critical analysis. In the overall structure of the book, I travel through the alchemists' five basic elements, looking at archetypes and stereotypes that resound in Earth, Fire, Air, Water and Space. My informing metaphor is the alchemists' effort to transform self into numen, dross into gold.

India, gouache, 19th century

In contemporary Western culture homosexuality signifies transformation – personal upheaval, social disruption, and spiritual change. We can refuse these meanings, and the journey, tasks and attainments that are suggested by a capacity for transformation. We can advocate for ordinariness, decline each special meaning, and look to the normalization of homosexuality for safety to live our mundane lives in peace. Or we can amplify the symbolic resonance of queer identities, explore and expand our capacities, and use these gifts to change the culture that would confine us.

Jung writes, "Not for a moment dare we succumb to the illusion that an archetype can finally be explained and disposed of. . . . The most we can do is to dream the myth onwards. . . ."[6] I write here to "dream the myth onwards." I speak of a "we" which history has constituted – we are the homosexuals. History constructs the meta-category of homosexuality, allowing us to claim identity across differences. Multiple, diverse and often antagonistic differences of sexuality, gender, race, culture and class are embraced by the category of homosexuality. In this sense, there is a global fellowship of homosexual people. History, language and culture present us with a stark differentiation between "us" and "them." Homosexuality requires of its advocates a kind of "strategic essentialism"[7] – we can use our identity with others to build alliances and create belongingness. In this sense, homosexual identity can be understood as an important social and historical aim, as well as an analytical tool. Stuart Hall writes that identities "are about using the resources of history, language and culture in the process of becoming rather than being: not 'who we are' or 'where we come from', so much as what we might become, how we have been represented and how that bears on how we might represent ourselves."[8]

In this book I write of *choosing* queer identity. We can use the history, language and culture that construct this identity to create new forms of being and new worlds. When I write of being queer, then, I am not writing of particular GLBTQ lives. Rather, I am giving attention to a cultural construct and locus of meaning that seems rich in content and capacity.

Queer, as I describe it here, precludes the closure implied by fixed and singular notions of identity. We each in queer community owe parallel allegiances to multiple identity positions. And people are forever whirling and turning from one sexual orientation to another. In recent years writers have explored the conflicted identities of lesbians who sleep with men, or transsexual men in gay relationships who become female and thereby straight. Certainly whenever anyone loudly claims to "be" heterosexual, we can hear the tiny, screeching voice of an inner homosexual. And homophobia is so fundamental to our culture, it is constitutive of any identity we lay claim to. We cannot live without an inner homophobe who wants to manage our options and strangle our dreams. As a queer person, I am meant to be marginalized and excluded from majority culture, and yet I also participate in telling the stories and constellating the identity by which being queer assumes its meanings. When I write of "we," I embrace queer identity in all its complexity. I call on what is queer in all people, however they conceive of their sexual orientation. Queer is, but is not only, the part of everyone that opens to the possibility of same-sex love. In this book, queer means the part of I that is an other, the one we glimpse in dreams. Bent on social transformation, queer is vulnerable, yet willing to risk. Queer is guided by inner yearnings instead of community consensus. Being queer is not inevitable, but it is possible, no matter who we love. This book is written to honour the aspects of anyone's life that can be explored and enjoyed through attention to the social construction of homosexuality. Being queer, as I see it, is nothing any homosexual is born to. It is a possibility we may – or may not – invent and discover, as we live with the socially reviled, yet culturally crucial concept of homosexuality.

Though this book is a very personal meditation, I imagine some ways it might be useful to others.

For those engaged in a personal journey of growth and discovery, I hope this opens a dressup trunk to play with. I find each chapter or aspect of *Orientation* can form a place for meditation and inspiration. I like to use, try on, enjoy and discard various facets of homosexuality as a personal pathway for spiritual growth.

In my work as a Somatic Sex Educator I find queer archetypes appear again and again in the erotic imagination of my clients (although most of them are heterosexually-identified). I encourage people to dance with queer myths and meanings. We can cherish the complexity they invite us discover, in the world and in ourselves.

Creative people may find, as I do, that attention to the images and archetypes surrounding queer identity can inspire new work, sometimes in unexpected ways. For example, the section of this book I call

"Water," with its flow of images and meditations on the nature and culture of water, informed my 2004 sculpture, *Water Dream / Water Memory*. In a Vancouver park I worked with a community to build a 400-foot long dry creekbed following the path of a buried stream. The environmental sculpture incorporates river rocks, riparian plants, and rocks engraved with a poem about water. The concept involved creating a tiny complex piece of nature to serve as habitat. The work proceeds directly from thinking nature through a queer point of view. It echoes an intricate, unseen and refused (queer) nature; it explores connections between blood, tears, constrained complexity (homosexuality), and a buried stream; it asks people to pay attention to the intersection between self and world (in a way that both evokes and proceeds from being queer).

For readers whose passion is for social justice, I hope this book enlivens the conversation. I am myself a passionate local activist. I have explored the implications of my view for political action throughout the book, and most particularly in the concluding chapter, "Stereotypes, Archetypes and Activism." In addition to the contemporary focus on civil rights, I would recuperate gay liberation, and continue to use queer as a social project. In recent years, GLBTQ activists have pushed for social tolerance of queer difference. Their work has had profound effects. I feel safer in my community and in my skin because of the legal and social reforms achieved by the civil rights movement. My gratitude is balanced by awareness that hate crimes have increased. An openly hostile "family-values" coalition has achieved significant political presence. Among the small majority of people who constitute civil society, prejudice may only be more secret. Fear and hatred of homosexuality may even be characterized by denial. The wish for our annihilation must be expressed politely, as a wish for our assimilation: "They are no different," or, "It makes no difference to me." The space between the toleration of difference and the annihilation of difference is easily bridged. Audre Lorde cautions, "Advocating the mere tolerance of difference . . . is the grossest reformism. It is a total denial of the creative function of difference in our lives."[9]

Pipe, early 19th century, unknown Haida artist, argillite. Portland Art Museum, Museum Purchase: Helen Thurston Ayer Fund, 43.18.2

This book is written to affirm and nourish queer difference. Love and laughter open our hearts to our capacities. Images and archetypes help us find the places of creativity and power in our history, community, lives and identities. As we carry the displaced needs and wishes of an entire culture, the otherness we are can form a dialectical opposition to the society that oppresses us. Without difference, there is no dialectic, and no possibility of social transformation. While we cannot escape or transcend homophobia, we can choose a way of conceiving self and world that is apposite and opposite. By inventing, exploring, preserving and proclaiming our difference, we enable creative change in society and in each heart.

In my view, queer can be so much more than sexual preference, psychological condition, and minority status. Queer is a way of being, a *Tao*, that can be practiced. It is a joy and a calling. Homosexuality allows us to redefine the scope of our souls. It is a way to embrace and repair the world. With every image, pattern and archetype we build into the web of nature and society, we make ourselves and the world more queer, and so at once more fabulous, more complicated, and more whole. [10]

Drawing by Aristide Maillol

Water

Water is the quintessential queer element. We are everywhere, in everything, like water.

Tides ebb and flood, linking continents. Blood circulates, continually replenished. Rivers flow to the sea, carving canyons into mountainsides. Water is constantly moving, and it is always there, as persistent as the inexplicable existence of same-sex love. Water flows to fit any shape. Its movement continues around, above or below any obstacle. At all times, in all conditions, we persist in our loving. We have no beginning. We have no end.

Water is threatened and endangered: ditched, diked, dammed, drained, poisoned. Yet nothing can live without water.

Water reflects and evokes our double, the watery one we ache for and cannot have. It is a symbol of this thirst. Water is the home of the great sea goddess, an angry lesbian image, and the salmon, whose impossible journey across the ocean and up the river is a homecoming that being queer proclaims. Rain nourishes the earth. Earth and water meet and mix in wetlands, the origin of life. The aquifer is an underground reservoir of cold, clear water.

Being queer, we stay close to the ground, like water. Water is our kinship with all life.

Frank Sutcliff, *Waterrats*, 1891.

The River

Salmon school up in small bays in the inlet, waiting for a rain. They have traveled halfway around the world since they were born in the gravel four-hundred miles upriver. Now they are back at the river mouth, and as soon as the rain comes they begin their incredible journey. Fighting against the current, they climb waterfalls and hurl themselves over rocks. Riding backeddies, resting in deep wells, exhausted and torn to shreds, they swim to their spawning ground.

Many die. Predators gather at the river, feasting bounteously. But all who live keep swimming against the current, going home.

Queer people are called to a journey like this. Like the salmon, we must go home, even when home seems impossible. Drawn irrevocably by our inner compass, listening only to our inmost images and instincts, we undertake this journey, almost hopeless against all odds. On the way, we need courage, faith, resilience, and plenty of luck. So many are destroyed. Yet age after age, perversely, we come home. We die, we are murdered, and yet we continually reconstitute the web of life. Swimming upstream, we are nevertheless the spirit of the river, its most telling inhabitant. Without our spawn, skeletons and skins, without our brilliant colors and our impossible journey, the river is emptied of magic and meaning. Like a salmon, or a shaman, each queer person leaves the realm of common sense to undertake a tortuous quest and a transformation: the journey with ecstasy – or Death – at its end and a return to life as its re-beginning. We come back with gifts. Perhaps we carry the capacity to speak with Death and the afterlife, with animal spirits and with gods.

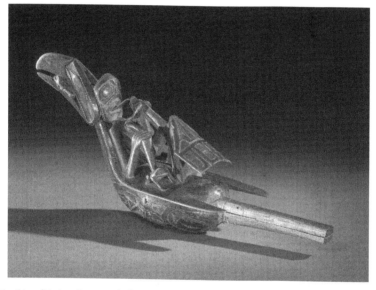

Tsimshian (Native American). Raven Rattle, 19th century. Wood, pigment, rattles, cotton twine, 5 1/2 x 14 x 4 in. (14.0 x 35.6 x 10.2 cm). Brooklyn Museum, Museum Expedition 1905, Museum Collection Fund, 05.588.7292. Creative Commons.
The rattle depicts a shaman on the back of a raven.

Hilary Stewart describes the "First Salmon Ceremony" by which the Salish people at Saanich welcomed the salmon returning to the river. Children all carried a salmon, holding the dorsal fin in their teeth. They stroked and soothed the fish as they traveled in a procession up from the water to the cooking fire, while the Ritualist sang thanks to the salmon.[1]

Severed from nature and the mythic dimensions of being, contemporary society would have it that salmon comes in tins. Without a sense of nature's generosity and power, people can grow materialistic and cynical. Even their dreams could stay individualistic and small – if it were not for the existence of GLBTQ people. We are the ones who dare depart the safe confines of a predictable life, and venture into a dangerous unknown. Our goal cannot be personal aggrandizement or social approval. We each move instead to grasp and live the fabulous wonder of an inborn self. Becoming queer means harkening to the gods' will, despite doubt and fear, in the face of innumerable obstacles. We swim upstream, impossible distances, against the odds, with only our inmost impulses to guide us. The incredible journey – to self-knowledge, to love and community – stands in drastic contrast to souls sunk in cynicism, rotting with surfeit, cowering in fear of imagined perils.

In a society without conscious myths, rites and sacraments to conjure the sacred and guide the soul to its calling, queer identity carries enormous power. GLBTQ people live the story of the hero. We each embody the archetypal pattern of the singular individual who, with improbable courage, finds and creates a home in a hostile world. There is an essential generosity, a call to community, in our story. Tyranny – including the tyranny of what is ordinary, expected, possible, and easy – overtakes any place without heroes to inspire rebellion.[2] Queer people are icons to all who would dare to risk despair for the sake of freedom. We make a place in the world for mythic struggle and transformation, when we endure punishment for the dream of love.

Thomas Eakins, *Swimming hole*. 1885, oil painting. Amon Carter Museum.

Fluidity

Queer identity is open and fluid, still best described as love and longing.
Although our bodies have been endlessly scrutinized and interrogated,
we cannot be contained. In other societies same-sex sexual experience
is enjoyed by one hundred percent of the population.[1] Nothing biological impedes the rampant reproduction of homosexuality. Yet we
are surrounded by "science" that aims to pin it down, to make of us
a minority who cannot help being what we are. Simon Levay, neuro-
scientist and author of *Queer Science*, notes that social acceptance of
homosexuals hinges on the belief that we are not like them. We cannot infect, subvert or seduce them because we are born that way and
they, emphatically, are not. Still there remains the lingering question
of whether, perhaps secretly, or unconsciously, they really are. Homosexuality is the identity that is always possible. Queer cannot finally be

fixed by difference. We can never really be said to stand opposite an other that constitutes our border and limit. We are everywhere. Ours is an identity that lurks inside, and might just rub the thighs of our fiercest enemies.

The scientists who puzzle over the ears of lesbians and the hypo-thalami of gay men[2] wonder how to identify the objects of their re-search. How does one search for a gay gene, without deciding just what constitutes homosexuality? Is homosexuality defined by practices or desires? Does the concept include only those who publicly describe themselves as queer, or does it also comprise those who hide, deny or equivocate? Does homosexuality describe all those who engage in same-sex sexual behaviors, even in sex-segregated spaces like prison, the military, logging camps, nunneries, and girls' schools, where same-sex sexuality is so widespread? What of those big, tough women and effeminate men who are married with children and grandchildren? In different social circumstances, would their gender dissonance be ex-pressed in homosexuality? And then there are the many people whose same-sex relationships are not sexual, but are still passionate and pri-mary. Is there anyone at all who can remain untouched by the fluid fact of homosexuality?

We are taught to assume that opposite-sex sexuality is the erot-ic preference of the normal, the majority. In the powerful 1980 es-say, "Compulsory Heterosexuality and Lesbian Existence," Adrienne Rich comments, "[heterosexuality] is an enormous assumption to have glided so silently into the foundations of our thought."[3] In fact, she notes and apparently proves with numerous examples of coercion and punishment, "heterosexuality may not be a 'preference' at all but some-thing that has to be imposed, managed, organized, propagandized, and maintained by force. . . ." Without the brutal imposition of gender roles, patriarchal powers, and opposite-sex sexuality, would there be one person who did not enjoy the magic and mystery of being queer?

In the 1980's – partially in response to Rich's influential essay – women opposing patriarchy seemed all to be privileging and professing lesbianism. For a short time, "lesbian-feminist" became a hyphenated identity, as if one never arrived without the other. In the 1990's "queer" achieved a similar kind of slipperiness, until the word almost managed to refuse and abandon its origins in homosexuality, and name everyone with the requisite gear. Homophobia sometimes poisoned these willful assumptions of almost-gay identities, as when lesbian-feminists called their butch-femme contemporaries unenlightened, or queer straights decried the essentialism of radical gays. Still, these are moments when homosexuality was purposefully embraced as a tool, a mask and a posture expressing social meanings. Perhaps it requires only a quixotic courage to identify oneself as queer, and then to use homosexuality as a source of knowledge and power.

Despite the fluidity of gay identities, and a suspicion that homosexuality may be "the primitive form of sexual longing,"[4] as Freud wrote in 1899, there is no denying that being queer is a radical form of existence. Where others submit to the same dull round of repetition and reproduction, we go by preference, astonishment, the surprise of desire. Instead of vanishing into predictable categories, GLBTQ people transform established patterns, seek new habitats and abandon others, live and thrive where it seems we cannot.

Our identity-with-homosexuality is derived through our kinship with one another. We seek and recall each other. The connection is magical, for we not only see in each other a present, kindred spirit, we know each other's past: our childhood as shy boys and bold girls who climbed trees and talked to butterflies. We know, as Harry Hay describes it, how we had to pull the green frog-skin of heterosexual conformity over ourselves to get through high school with a full set of teeth.[5] And how, if we are not yet free of it, the fairy prince or princess that we are is there beneath the skin, waiting to be awakened with a kiss. "I do not doubt I am to meet you again, / I am to see to it that I do not lose you," sings Walt Whitman.[6] Queer is an irrevocable bond. Ours is no subcultural community where people share a heritage and common culture. More of an interculture, we are everywhere, extending into the dominant culture in so many ways, on so many trajectories, that queer could be the glue that holds the mosaic of subcultures together. Being queer means building identity across and between us, bridging differences of sexuality, gender, race, culture and class. This form of community is chosen and achieved, not simply given. Where most communities gain their strength and structure by rejecting the other, we accept each pilgrim who announces their affinity.

Jean Matheus (1590 – 1672), *Hermaphrodite et Salmacis*. illustration for Ovid's Metamorphosis. 1651. Wikimedia.

We are everywhere, and yet we each have to literally fabricate ourselves and each other as queer people in hostile environments. The love which invents queer identity is nothing ordinary. It is tough and daring, gracious as a drag-queen, fierce as a bull-dagger, and just as astonishing as a woman-loving-woman, a man-loving-man. Through homosexuality we make an extraordinary leap into a sex with no other abjected and opposite.

Surely everyone has the capacity for homosexuality, but few have the courage. No one who is not – or not-yet – queer can grasp this. In 1972 Martha Shelley writes, "I will tell you what we want, we radical homosexuals: not for you to tolerate us, or to accept us, but to understand us. And that you can only do by becoming one of us. We want to reach the homosexuals entombed in you, to liberate our brothers and sisters locked in the prisons of your skulls."[7] Liberating this inner homosexual means something different from tasting the forbidden fruit of same-sex sexual experience. There is not really a question of whether you have or have not. There is the question of whether, from the endless possible responses to the (universal?) experience of same-sex desire, you choose love. Instead of living a bounded and defended sexual identity, being queer means having open, fluid identifications with other who are like us, or who may become so, or who may once have been so. Will Roscoe writes of the Navaho third-gender *nádleehí*, "the one who is (constantly) changing.[8] Adding a third and fourth term to the binary system of gender, queer upsets the balance and invites motion and change.

Science would like to prove that homosexuality is a permanent, pathological state. Western culture imagines us as a distinct minority. But someone completely improbable is always coming out, while others freeze up and go back in. Queer precludes closure. If the GLBTQ community has integrity, it is like a watershed. Gary Snyder describes the watershed as "the first and last nation, whose boundaries, though subtly shifting, are inarguable. . . . The watershed gives us a home, and a place to go upstream, downstream, and across in."[9] The queer nation has this character. It is continually taking in and letting go, the way rain swells the creeks and streams, and the river flows into the sea. Of course queer people can be just as intent as anyone else on vanishing into predictable categories: gender, sexual identity, family, race, class, nation, occupation. Yet the water is still there, singing its secrets. Being queer gives us a kinship with all life, like water. And even when ditched, diked, dammed, and filled with garbage, water will find its way down.

Caravaggio, *Medusa*, 1597

The Sea

The Inuit goddess who lives at the bottom of the sea was once a woman who refused to marry. Her angry father chopped off her hands, which fell into the water and miraculously transformed into seals, walruses, and whales. Sedna herself fell to the ocean floor, where she lives forever, guarding the creatures who came from her fingers. She is the most powerful goddess, with authority over our destiny. Her wild, matted hair is thick with the blood of animals killed by hunters and fishers. The wicked deeds of humans infest her hair like lice.

Sedna tells what happens when we do not acquiesce to woman's social role and her place in the symbolic order. When we are lesbians, we are punished and expelled from human society. Literally or symbolically, we sink out of sight. When we will not serve men, our hands are cut off. Our work is inhibited, our independence crippled, our capacities denied. But lesbians are unstoppable. Amputated hands become sea creatures – magical, mysterious, independent souls in their own right. Fingers slip deep inside the smooth, wet darkness beneath the surface of things. Thumbs come up for air, and dive again into deeper water.

Despite Sedna's powers she is infested by human wickedness, and so are we, the lesbians. Though we are infinitely deep and immeasurably wide, we cannot ignore the mean measures of our origins. We mostly come from families where ordinary life separates human beings into men and women. We do not fit in. We know the preposterous quality of sexual difference. We see the coercion masked by it. We each spill some of the blood shed in enforcing it.

We see how little girls are prevented from becoming active, desiring subjects. We experience the same perils that convince women to assume the passive aims of femininity. We lick the very wounds that keep them yoked to fear. And yet we are not and cannot ever be women. Monique Wittig comments, "The refusal to become (or to remain) heterosexual always meant to refuse to become a man or a woman, consciously or not." She continues, "what makes a woman is a specific social relation to a man . . . ."[1] Woman is one element of a two-gender system – created by her envy, her service, her powerlessness. Lesbians escape this fate. Yet we cannot escape being marked, like a woman, by the designation of sexual difference. It is the phantom pain inside our amputated limbs.

It seems lesbians are bound to work tirelessly for women's freedom. We are often the foremost providers of liberating services to women. Wherever there are battered women's support services, birth control and abortion services, and women's cultural services, there are lesbians. And yet, Wittig writes, "it would be incorrect to say that lesbians associate, make love, live with women, for 'woman' has meaning only in heterosexual systems of thought and heterosexual economic systems."[2] In Chinese calligraphy, as in American advertising, "woman" is written as "person with a broom" or "person with a son."[3] Wittig argues that 'woman,' like 'slave,' is a concept that cannot be rehabilitated and 'lesbian' is proof of its insufficiency. Our refusal of the social consequences of being women constructs an escape route that can be followed. Or women can sit tight, confined by the awful restraints – or perhaps even placated by the meager rewards – of being female.

Man assumes all the power in our culture, but who would be a man? Certainly not lesbians. Gay men, too, escape this fate of the master and his vulnerabilities. "Man" cannot be without "woman" to guarantee his subjectivity by her service, his wealth by her work, his authority by her abjection. The whole creaking edifice of gender cracks and crumbles when we undermine it by being queer.

Lesbian and gay existence shifts sexual difference from the realm of biology, where male and female interact in lifeless unity. Slipping out of sight, we prove an alternative. We show that male and female are not facts that quietly and irreversibly emerge from the realm of nature. These are social identities, carved out brutally by history. They are enforced and exploitative economic relationships. Homosexuality demonstrates opposition and invites resistance.

All our lives, we hear from the homophobes that women who love women are not real women, and men who love men cannot be men. Instead of, or as well as, claiming the opposite, we can celebrate this truth. Queer means we withdraw our consent from the sex-gender system. We refuse its processes and values. When love draws us back to the constraints of ordinary life, we need not forget our capacities. Does it constitute a service, if we always keep silent? Exiled and escaped, we learn to dwell outside, beyond, above and below the opposite poles of sexual difference. In place of the dreary, static identities assumed by male and female, we become both and neither. We ebb and flood as an entirely different element, with the complex, certain rhythm of the sea.

Jules-Cyrille Cave, *Narcissus*, 1890.

Surfaces

"Only the shallow know themselves."

– OSCAR WILDE[1]

"Invert," the word derived from the Latin *in* (in) and *vertere* (to turn), names the action of turning inward. And this is not any ordinary self-reflection, but an in-turning that turns things upside down and inside out. The noun "invert" names one who is transformed by inversion – who else but the homosexual.

Being queer is a call to inversion, an in-turning that leads us to quiet places in nature, where still, clear water upturns the known world. And if a wandering youth is thirsty for a taste of this inverted world, where all is soft, deep and unfamiliar, he might catch sight of his own watery soul. Narcissus finds an image reflected in the dark surface of a hidden pond – a self who he thinks is someone else – and he falls in love. The boy he yearns for is not the familiar image of himself he could find in a bright-lit mirror. It is a surprising, unfamiliar self – fluid, secret, soulful.[2]

Narcissus' love for the boy he finds deep in the forest, in the untouched pool of still, clear water, can be described as an inversion of the ordinary self-consciousness that can be acquired through mirrors. Psychoanalyst Jacques Lacan describes the mirror-stage as formative of self-consciousness. In the brittle plane of a mirror, a child sees only surfaces. Reflections there say nothing of bodily fluids, organic needs, and interior functions. All the eye perceives in the mirror is an "I" who appears to be whole, complete, and independent.[3] While still "sunk in motor incapacity and nursling dependence," a child overcomes fear by assuming an identity with the insentient object he or she appears to be, in the mirror. The "I" is formed in this mirror-stage as a self-consciousness that is separate and self-sufficient. "I" forgets fear and danger. "I" repudiates knowledge of time and space, where we are interwoven with an intricate web of life. Yet no one has blood and breath apart from this. So "I" must stay trapped in paranoid structures. "I am" always poses (historically, linguistically) as a self-sufficient entity, disavowing identity with what it lacks. All that is other becomes viewed as inessential. The subject inhabits a negatively characterized world of objects. Jacques Lacan describes this "mirror stage" as a misrecognition that comes to characterize the ego in all its structures. He calls it a "knot of imaginary servitude that love must always undo again, or sever."[4]

Heterosexuality is one way to keep this self-sufficient self-consciousness going. "Man" and "Woman" are other and opposite, separate, distinct, composed of rejected attributes, negatively characterized. In relationship "he" and "she" function as mirrors to one another, offering up superficial images and reinforcing paranoid disavowals of fear and mortal destiny. Within the patriarchal social structures that surround and confound us, "woman" acts as object to his subject. She guarantees his power by her service. He stays trapped in the crippling misrecognition of his self-sufficiency. And perhaps he is also trapped in unconscious envy of her privileged access to feeling and to powerlessness.

Loving someone of the same sex, we cannot stay in comfortable assumptions of difference. We recognize our identity with our lovers. We see and want our double, our self. But this is not the mirror-self, appearing whole, complete, and independent. We catch a glimpse of the fluid, soulful self – weeping, urinating, defecating, hungry, thirsty, readily shattered, impossibly needy – in our lover's eyes, arms, and asshole.

When two women or two men love each other, no female (or feminized) object stands opposite a male (or masculinized) subject. No one guarantees his power by her service. Paul Monette describes "the challenge two men fucking [make] to the slave laws of the patriarchy. . . . the exchange of power, the wild circle of top and bottom."[5] Two men together make a "wild circle" of subject and object, dependence and independence, separation and merging, passivity and power. Being queer makes it possible to acknowledge strength and weakness, authority and abjection, in a wild erotic round. Difference does not derive from indifference. Objective insufficiency need not be cast into an abyss inside self-knowledge; it can be used, played with, cared for and loved as an aspect of both self and other.

The anxious self-certainty of ordinary self-consciousness can only be achieved by the transcendence of objectivity. It is the objective truth of separation and independence that guarantees one's insufficiency and need. An alternative consciousness lives in the world of objects: organic, endangered bodies; trees and rain; food and water; books and music; blood and skin. Grief, hunger, love and laughter illuminate – at times with unendurable clarity – the gap between individual and indivisible life. Instead of claiming transcendent self-certainty through the repudiation of risk and dependence, being queer means we can listen to uncertainty and live in cognizance of incompletion. The endangered self, wanting what it does not have, can only be loved through inversion.

In unique relation with the dynamics of self-consciousness, queer people can claim rich capacities and sensibilities. We can want more than the self-sufficient subject could ever dream of not-having. We can acknowledge abject need without surrendering all power. Despite and because of our objective limits, we can take a chance on love.

Pere Colom, *Comunicación Sexual,* 1996. Polaroid Transfer.

The Aquifer

Exploring homosexual orientation is a journey underground, to the realm of silence and uncreated things. There are no easy assumptions and predetermined projects. Each queer person begins by asking what it means to be queer. Who am I? What am I here for? Is there a buried history? A higher purpose? A special gift for art and music? Or is queer something one can refuse to be, like James Baldwin, who puts it down to "love, in the tough and universal sense of quest, and daring and growth"?[1] Homosexuality is marked by this existential uncertainty, a passionate awareness of personal responsibility, a need to call into being both self and community.

Homosexuality means we cannot live an unexamined life. And here, with respect to all the queer people who do, I will say again that I am speaking of homosexuality as a social construct, and not describing particular queer lives. In social and cultural terms, homosexuality is de-naturalized, set apart as a problem which requires at least an opinion if not a solution. "The love that once dared not speak its name now can't keep its mouth shut," Time Magazine opined after the Stonewall Rebellion in 1969.[2] Homosexuality is the sexuality which must be described, hushed up, explained, claimed, denied, celebrated and studied. Every GLBTQ person forges an identity inside this welter of words and silences. Each one of us is invited, if not forced, to scrutinize history, personal feelings and the structure of society before we admit to homosexuality.

Becoming queer engages us in an archetypal journey beneath the surface of things. We go down into the dark, deep immensity of the Underworld. We follow the yellow brick road to the Emerald City.[3] Like Orpheus, we create unearthly music. Like Dorothy, we will make irreplaceable friends. We are bound to meet death, and our own fear of death, as we subvert the inevitability of breeding. We wrestle with the bad witch, cajole the ineffectual wizard, and contest the Underworld for our beloved. We integrate despised and fearful aspects of female power and male vulnerability. We encounter our own failure. We face self-doubt and find, to our great surprise, we already have the courage, heart and brains that we've been seeking. Finally we click our red heels together, and say "There's no place like home."

Home is homosexuality – an underground reservoir of cool, sweet water. In her 1974 sociological study, Carol Warren writes, "The gay world, because it is stigmatized and set apart, is one that demands total identification. Thus a person who affiliates with the community and accepts gay identity possesses a rarity in contemporary life: a total and all-encompassing core of existence by which to answer the question Who am I?"[4] Being queer embraces all of who we are. It answers the heart's deepest yearnings for place and identity.

To reach the aquifer one must travel alone, beneath norms, expectations and established forms of relationship. Once we drink there, we are irrevocably changed. Homosexuality alters the form and content of our relationship with whatever other communities, religious affiliations, class, race and family alliances claim us. It calls for new social forms and a radical re-visioning of human capacities. If there is love between men, how will armies function?[5] If women are hard and men are penetrable, what is gender? Will the patriarchy fissure and split apart? Michel Foucault comments, "We have to understand that with our desires go new forms of relationships, new forms of love, new forms of creation. Sex is not a fatality; it is a possibility for creative life."[6]

Queer is achieved by the lonely undertaking of a mythic journey. Yet our identity is derived from the hard give and take of our connections with one another. Queer community gives us a name and a home, though it scarcely exists. No institutions support it; no place defines it; no spokesperson can represent it. The community is "an ephemeral, woven network of belonging" (Aaron Betsky)[7] that depends on our participation. Orientation continually weaves both self and community.

Homosexuality makes us acutely sensitive. We need to be open and empathic enough to find our way in and then brave enough to find our way down. We move inside the maw of fear, past all the possibilities and expectations we were born to, guided by feeling, going on faith. It is a journey home to love. Each queer person can claim and embrace a self that balances sensitivity with courage, delicacy with strength. Concomitantly, we learn to have and to hold each other. Love that is big enough to admit us can also admit what is awful and incomplete about us. We hold on, even to the terrible and tedious aspects of the beloved, inside this space of radical openness. We hold all the glittering immensity we can be and give birth to.

Our passions take us down into the secret heart of the world. Inside the dark earth, down deep below the surfaces, we find this untapped aquifer of queer meanings.

Moche vessel, from the Museo Larco, in Lima, Peru. Photo: Pfrishauf.

Slime

Wetlands are the slimy in-between places where earth and water meet and mix. They are edges, ecotones, places of vast diversity. They stink with the sharp, sulphurous smell of life's beginning. Light transforms into life. Every tablespoon of water contains millions of organisms: phytoplankton, zooplankton, bacteria. Wetlands stabilize soil and clean water. They are vital habitat. The history of European settlement in North America is a history of the devastation and elimination of wetlands. Estuaries were buried, and dredged to create harbours. Bogs were drained, marshes were filled, and swamps were turned into farms and suburbs. The fur trade eliminated millions of acres of beaver-built wetlands. Water was diverted, dammed, ditched, and captured for irrigation, sanitation and electric power.

The European adventurers hated slime. Jean-Paul Sartre describes it thus: "Slime is the agony of water. It presents itself as a phenomenon in the process of becoming; it does not have the permanence within change that water has. . . . Nothing testifies more clearly to its ambiguous character as a 'substance between two states' than the slowness with which the slimy melts into itself."[1] White, Western man wants clear edges and sharp delineations between land and water, differences as obvious as those between Christian and Savage, man and nature. Where native North American cultures hone capacities for kinship and transformation, European psychic and social organization relies on the difference and distance between self and other, male and female, human and animal, us and them. When one state melts into another, what might not be destabilized by the stink and slime of intense diversity?

The repression of diversity is the hallmark of western culture. And yet the West, with its characteristic racism, sexism, imperialism and exploitation of nature, is the birthplace of homosexuality. Inasmuch as homosexuality is a constellation of meanings with an historically-specific resonance, the genesis of its social construction is embedded in Western culture and Judeo-Christian tradition. While same-sex sexuality exists everywhere, throughout nature and around the world, the possibility of being queer – of having a soul and a life shaped by homosexuality – began in Europe and bloomed in America. The concept of homosexuality is still irrelevant in a few far corners of the world, where family life is compulsory. In countries and cultures where men and women meet to enjoy the delights of same-sex sexuality, and then must return to the responsibilities of marriage and family life, homosexuality does not assume the fabulous meanings it has in Western culture. In countries and cultures where same-sex sexuality is an aspect of the shaman's identity, or is a universally-practiced initiatory rite, there are other constellations of meanings than when same-sex sexual relationships are named and stigmatized as homosexual.

Looking at the historical development of homosexual identity in Europe from the Middle Ages to the Enlightenment, Rudi Bleys[2] charts the shift from describing a "ubiquitous, ever-luring sodomitical sin" to an effeminate and sexually passive minority. By the mid-18th century sodomy "was increasingly perceived as a characteristic of someone else, as something alien to oneself, in sum, as a sign of difference within the boundaries of Europe."[3] The homosexual takes shape from this sodomite, as the despised other inside the dream of white western man.

Historically, the construction of homosexuality intersected with the construction of racialized others. European adventurers refused conversation with non-western lifeways, economies, sex-gender systems and forms of government. Instead, the 'savage' was conjured. The same pattern of repudiation and differentiation that created homosexuality served to create race and whiteness. Even the same metaphors were used. Savages were naked and brutish. Characterized as effeminate or hyper-masculine, savages had a propensity for same-sex passions. The death of millions of Native Americans from diseases brought – at times deliberately – by Europeans was attributed to divine retribution for the sin of sodomy.[4]

Stuart Hall writes, "Racism, of course, operates by constructing impassable symbolic boundaries between racially constituted categories, and its typically binary system of representation constantly marks and attempts to fix and naturalize the difference between belongingness and otherness."[5] The racialized other is marked and fixed over there, in the Third World, or the ghetto, at the margin. Yet homosexuality exists – not only as an aspect of the savage's pathologized sexuality, but inside the boundaries of whiteness. Homosexuality is the slime inside white racial identity – an undifferentiated element with an ambiguous character that slides between states, "a phenomena in the process of becoming" (Sartre).

The white body is a body of knowledge – history, memory and discursive practices that claim entitlement through the differentiation of self from other, subject from object, insider from outsider. Ruth Frankenberg observes that the white self does not pre-exist the production of others. It is constituted in the process of constructing a range of bounded others, relegated to service, ghettos, reservations and distant corners of the world. Homosexuality interrupts and destabilizes whiteness. Like the slime and stink of a marshy wetland underlying a coastal city, the despised other flows just beneath the surface of a badly-constituted self.

The psychological and social processes of domination, disavowal and wounding create the self-other binary that white western man lives inside of. Moving to control and objectify every living thing, he achieves a false differentiation that sees only polarity and opposition where there is mutuality and interdependence. He aspires to achieve his fictive identity by denying, betraying and inflicting violence on every part of self and world that cannot be called both masculine and white. Homosexuality undermines him. Lewis Gordon explores the metaphors. "Consider a white man. Being pure Presence, he is equated with manliness *in toto*. The manly, or masculine, is in fact a figure of denial, a being who attempts to close all its holes and become pure, sealed flesh in search of holes. From the perspective of such a being, all holes are elsewhere; he doesn't even have an anus. . . ."[6] Yet there are homosexual men, beside or inside him, who open to the pleasures of penetration. There are homosexual women who won't play the hole to his phallus. Homosexuality forms an integral – and yet always denied – part of white Western history and consciousness, in a world that is dominated by its power and violence.

Homosexuality persists in the space between self and other, inside the tension, out along the distances. Queer people occupy this slimy place of change and becoming. We may find here an opportunity to destabilize race and gender systems. But the capacity of homosexuality to change and challenge the self-other binary is constrained by the image of homosexuals as a biologically-constituted minority. Minority status absolves the majority of the capacity for homosexuality

Hans Burgkmair, *The Fight in the Forest*, pen and black ink on laid paper, National Gallery of Art, Washington, Ailsa Mellon Bruce Fund

It contains the contagion, obviates the lure, and obscures the content of homosexual identity. Rudi Bleys notes that 19th century discourse applies the minority model only to depictions of white western homosexuality. When describing other cultures, same-sex sexuality is considered a "characterizing trait" and an obvious sign of a people's lower status on the evolutionary scale. "Presenting indigenous homosexuality as a 'minority trait' . . . would acquit a majority, which went against the imperatives of racialist rhetoric."[7] Minority status allows white gays and lesbians to be abject others only with regard to their sexual orientation, while they assume the privileges and perils of whiteness in other aspects of their lives.

The contemporary gay civil rights movement claims that homosexuality is a natural deviation from normal life – no more threatening to the general culture than cheese. Queer people can abjure the power of their difference, and make a claim to legitimacy – based on the certain fact that same-sex sexuality is the natural preference of a biologically-constituted minority. They thereby ensure that, as a minority, they always only stay marginal to the majority sexuality and its culture. Queer activists and scholars show that homosexuality is not, or at least not only, a fixed minority identity that we either are or are not. Being queer means using the transgressive capacities of homosexuality to query the cultural, economic and social processes by which any minority is constituted.

Jamake Highwater condemns the "self-defeating process of naturalization"[8] that turns homosexuals into people "who cannot transgress, but must await permission to step over the line." He writes, "It is this normalization of homosexuality that turns outcasts into clones of those who made them outcasts in the first place."[9] He urges us to use the power of our difference. Alienation and marginalization are not just difficulties to overcome. They are great adventures. They are instruments of analysis. We learn to scrutinize and contest boundaries, to mine them for pleasures and open them to possibilities. Homosexuality opens up the space between self and other, male and female, us and them. Queer leads to deep resources and dangerous meanings.

Homosexuality may be the one good thing Western history and culture has proposed. It calls us to write a new history and make a new culture that includes the many colours and variegated histories of same-sex passions. In every corner of the world, people are responding to the lure and taking up the promise of homosexuality. The International Gay and Lesbian Association has 350 member groups on all five continents. Queer is a way of being so flexible and fluid, it gathers indigenous homosexualities into an international movement.

Being queer can function as a radical critique of colonial morals. Homosexuality constitutes a transgression of sex roles and family expectations. It is a joyful form of resistance to tyranny. We are called in a multitude of ways to love and to life that will destabilize the regime of power and difference, the disavowal and wounding, that white racial supremacy has naturalized.

Ancient petroglyghs in Bohuslan, Sweden, early first milleneum. showing the shamans in
erotic rituals. photo: Mehdi Naimi

Earth

We are earth. Earth is the lover. Earth is the body of us.

Earth germinates seed and nourishes the roots of plants. It receives all and gives even more bounteously, taking nothing but our mortal bodies for itself. Inside the darkness of the earth lies all that is dead and gone, and all that will become.

Earth is the image of the whole planet, Gaia, the complex entity that is our world. Origin, original goddess, nurturing womb and home: earth is the woman we love, when we are lesbians. The man-spirit of earth is also gay, mortal tree-god, androgynous son of the virgin mother.

Earth is soil, dark mystery. Being gay, we can admit the darkest corners of our hearts. Earth is the complexity and energy of wildness. We are the wild ones. Wild is who we are and where we are at home.

Earth is unconscious knowing: the energy of roots snaking through the dirt and mouth seeking clit to suck. Hand pushes into us; child pushes out; green shoots push through the soil in spring. Intuitive knowing, born in dreams and yearning, connects us magically with our lovers and our world.

Fifty-three stations of the Tokaido: Fukuroi station. From 'shunga' Tokaido series: attributed to Utagawa Hiroshige 1840, 9¼" x 6".

Wildness

"The most alive is the wildest."

-HENRY DAVID THOREAU[1]

"The mass of men lead lives of quiet desperation," writes Henry David Thoreau. "From the desperate city you go to the desperate country, and have to console yourself with the bravery of minks and muskrats."[2] On the one hand, the city prevents wildness, buries it, paves it over and cuts it out. On the other hand, in the desperate country, nature exists as spectacle. There wildness can be admired, but not lived. Thoreau envisions a different way of living, possessed of the energy and complexity of wildness. In his journal, he describes the dream of a community of friends: "I have glimpses of a serene friendship-land, and know the better why brooks murmur and violets grow."[3]

For Susan Griffin, in the wild, erotic conclusion of Woman and Nature, lesbian sex is how we live with nature, inside its urgencies, singing its songs:

"I could kiss your bones, put my teeth in you . . . I chew, beautiful one, I am in you . . . I have no boundary . . . I am perished in light, light filling you. . .carrying you out, through the roofs of our mouths, the sky, the clouds, bursting, raining. . . dispersed over the earth, into the soil, deep, deeper into you, into the least hair on the deepest root in this earth, into the green heart flowing, into the green leaves and they grow . . . ."4

Love, joy, passion, friendship, the exchange of fluids without the assignment of roles, pleasure without possession: while others act out their dreary routines in the social and symbolic order, queer is a call to wildness.

In the *Epic of Gilgamesh*, written down near 2100 B.C., same-sex love is identified with wildness. Gilgamesh is a king with a restless heart. In his discontent, he keeps his people working, building mighty walls and high towers. He leads them into war. Gilgamesh is the type of restless, ruthless man who still is everywhere. The thick walls he wants to seal his city off from the outside world, the high towers that display his power, his aggressivity against the forest people and his own subjects – it is easy to diagnose the desperation. Gilgamesh is missing something vital. All his offense and over-achievement is compensatory. What he needs, the gods decide, is one who is equal to him: his other, his double, a friend. The gods send Gilgamesh a lover – to teach him humility, to be a true companion. Enkidu is a hairy wild man who sucks the milk of wild animals. The forest is his home. Gilgamesh takes Enkidu to the palace, and gives him kingly food and clothing. The two men love each other passionately, but Enkidu cannot stay long in the city. He leaves for the wilderness, and Gilgamesh follows. Forsaking all his wealth and power, Gilgamesh pursues his beloved friend. They live together in the forest, becoming more and more dear to one another.

Albrecht Dürer, (1471–1528), *The Men's Bath*, 1496/97, Woodcut on cream laid paper, 15.43 in, x 11.14 in, Art Institute of Chicago. Wikimedia.

The *Epic of Gilgamesh* can be read as a drama of the soul called to going wild. Wild means undomesticated, impatient of restraint, fierce, crazy, eager with desire, free. Wildness is life energy, the intricate wisdom of natural systems, instinct, anima (breath, soul). Call it what you will, it calls us – out and away from domestic spheres and human settlements, into the forest, down to the water, up the mountainside. Through homosexuality, we partake of this wild nature.

For centuries, same-sex lovers have called each other "friends." Our love mixes us up instead of pinning us down; it is the amity of equals

instead of the enmity of opposites. We live despite the thousand prohibitions and permissions that enforce what a man is and what a woman is. Where we are, friendship is possible. We make space for each
other, and it is space where we can be all we are becoming. Love lets
us listen to a wild heart, find a voice to sing with, stretch our wings.
Friendship calls us away from the city. The walls around us open. Towers seem trivial. What matters now? I / Thou. A friend evokes our own
wild nature, demonstrates our kinship with plants and animals, carries
us home. Home is outside the marriage, away from the marketplace,
in the skin of a lion. Apart from the social order that presses us into
service, love brings us to life.

   "Family" is a word derived from the Latin *famulus*, meaning "servant." The word connotes obedience. The word "friendship" evolves
from the Anglo-Saxon *freond*, meaning "love." "Friendship – such a
boundless desire." The *Homomonument* in Amsterdam honors homosexual experience with these words by the Dutch poet Jacob Israël
de Haan.[5] Without the borders and customs agents, tariffs and duties
of straight norms and gender expectations, friendship is boundless.
We can soar, dive, and journey dark and deep – into the wildness of
the world.

George Catlin (1796-1872), *Dance to the Berdache*. Drawn while on the Great Plains, among the Sac and Fox Indians, the sketch depicts a ceremonial dance to celebrate the two-spirit person.

Dirt

"Homosexuality is not natural," claimed parliamentarian Roseanne Skoke in the Canadian House of Commons. "It is immoral and it is undermining the inherent rights and values of our Canadian families and it must not and should not be condoned."[1] With their hatred known as opinion, homophobes almost always begin thus – "unnatural!" is their most common invective. Where do they find a nature to confirm them? They must know nothing of mud or marsh, creek or ocean – nothing even of their own wild hearts. To believe that homosexuality is unnatural, they need stay completely unfamiliar with the world outside – or within – where homosexuality is as common as dirt.

When homophobes call us "unnatural," the nature they imagine is simple and desolate. It reflects only their own limited options. They think animals and even plants are always either male or female, and driven by a reproductive imperative. They dream that each species is bent on competition, engaged in a battle for survival that pits every life form against each other. They describe ants, swans, chimpanzees and flowers as if they have no moral life, no culture, and of course, no homosexuality.

Careful observation of nature yields another story. Birds do not come paired, male and female, as they do in bird books. They come in same-sex groups of three, five, and fifty. Bears and whales are among the many animals that form male and female same-sex pair bonds. They often raise adopted offspring. There is drag and performance in nature, as when a male hummingbird courts another male. He flies slowly back and forth, pivoting his body from side to side, flashing bright orange mouth lining and facial stripes.[2] Cock-of-the-rock, a South American bird, performs ritual dancing ceremonies for males and females.[3] There is excess and abundance in the ripening of fruit and the impossible genesis of phytoplankton. There is mercy, as trees make air to breathe, and rains nourish the earth. Plants make potent medicines for animals and us. Birch trees act as nurse trees for new-born Douglas Firs, sharing sugars through their roots.[4] There is art and artifice in nature: beehive, bird's nest, the figure-eights run by a female deer to arouse another doe. Sexes are not so opposite. There are many single-sex varieties of fish, lizards, snakes and salamanders. One all-female species of salamander has survived four million years.[5] Certain species of fish change their gender through their life cycle, or when social circumstances demand it, restructuring both brains and genitalia from male to female and vice versa.[6] Being queer, we are called to enter and partake of this world of nature, around and within us. We can see it clearly, in all its perversity and diversity. We can see and celebrate strangeness in the world and in ourselves.[7] It is at least a beginning, from which we can work to forge an intimate and restorative relationship with the natural world.

The homophobes have no beginning, no place from which to enter. To be and remain homophobic, they have to stay ignorant of complexity. They can never live with nature, singing its songs. Yet their homophobia can be seen to express a yearning for nature, along with a distance from it. It is a desperate, peculiar way to claim an affinity with the wild. They imagine that heterosexuality is natural through claiming homosexuality is not. Animals have nothing to say to them, but nevertheless, they claim a kinship. They imagine birds and bees are heterosexual, like them. They see the forest as scenery, or a resource. They will never be at home there. Still, they can feel their lives affirmed by its processes. They imagine each species engaged in competition, and bent on reproduction ... so unlike the homosexuals. Homophobia imbues their awful, empty lives with magic naturalness. They assert a secure place for themselves and their values in the unfolding world, just by hating homosexuals.

On the other hand, enlightened democrats may claim that homosexuals are part of nature. Don't blame gays and lesbians, they say. Queer folk are only victims of Mother Nature's caprice. Fuelled with righteous certainty, they imagine the telling question: Why would anyone ever choose to be homosexual, when it occasions so much misery and loss? The notion that queer is a joy and a calling is anathema to the democrats. The democrats manage to hold the same dim view of nature as the homophobes, though giving grudging admittance to homosexuality. But it is hard to weave us into the culture of nature, without changing the colours and the pattern. Hence "the cause" is madly pursued. Is homosexuality an adaptation, a substitution, an aberration, a consequence? Is there a cure? Simply affirming that homosexuality exists throughout nature requires a reconceptualization of natural systems.[8] It asks that we recognize multiplicity and mutability, magic and mystery.

The homophobe and the democrat want to live in a world ordered by scarcity (competition) and functionality (reproductive usefulness). We can begin to see it whole. Inside and outside, the world is wild. In all its intricate and unseen process, nature is alive with miracles and wonder.

France, c. 1920. Photographer unidentified.

Money

"Fags Doom Nations," the Westboro Baptist Church proclaims in its picketing ministry. Sure enough, "We are everywhere," loving across borders and passionately claiming community with multicultural expressions of same-sex love. Just as the world economy gathers all into its grip, more and more people make homosexuality a public choice and guiding aspect of their lives. While free trade agreements and information oligarchies render nations obsolete, the international queer community develops an infrastructure that is strong and visible.

Same-sex passion has always existed, throughout history and throughout nature. Being homosexual is different from this. The public voices and private lives of contemporary queers have no exact historical precedent. We have made homosexual desire into a personal identity and a global community. Queer shapes our lives and our souls.

In the 6th Century B.C. Sappho wrote beautiful and frankly sexual poems addressed to girls and women. But the lovers of this most famous Lesbian were not "lesbians" themselves. Sappho is thought to have run a school where girls were educated before they married. Their lives as wives may have included interludes of same-sex passion. Greek men of the period were expected to pursue sexual attachments to young men. But this "homosexuality" did not typically interfere with gender systems or matrimony. Even an acknowledged predisposition to same-sex attachments did not become an identity or pose an alternative way of life.

Among the Sambian people of New Guinea, boys become men by years of ingesting the semen of older boys and men. At about eight years old, a male child is separated from his mother and the world of women, and his initiation into the fellowship of men begins. Every day until puberty he sucks the cocks of older boys and men. After puberty his cock is sucked by a new group of younger boys. Finally, he becomes manly enough to marry.[1]

Sambian homosexuality is a constitutive element in a two-gender system. Because all men enjoy same-sex sexuality, no man can *be* homosexual. Same-sex passions are confined to predictable parameters – enjoyable, but unremarkable. Only in contemporary capitalist cultures does homosexuality represent as an alternative way of being.

Looking at the various manifestations of same-sex love in other times and places can give colour and texture to contemporary queer identities. But the possibility and promise of homosexuality has never been so thrilling as it is today. Queer passions do not fit into the interstices of the patriarchal family, the two-gender system, and the endless repetition of hereditary privilege. Homosexuality creates an antonym to expected life ways and historic forms of social organization.

For the possibility of queer identity to flourish, we need something like the material conditions that capitalism provides – wage labor unattached to family and fealty. John D'Emilio argues that there are and will be more and more people who identify as homosexuals, as capitalism creates a material basis for personal autonomy. He writes, "Only when individuals began to make their living through wage labour [in the second half of the 19th century], instead of as parts of an interdependent family unit, was it possible for homosexual desire to coalesce into a personal identity – an identity based on the ability to remain outside the heterosexual family and to construct a personal life based on attraction to one's own sex."[2]

Capitalism is scary. It rips people from their roots, alienates them from their work, dissolves languages and cultures in a tendency to globalization. It promotes individualism and individuality, as it brings workers into competition with each other. It is always seeking the lowest wage and the highest profit. Capitalism excises the heart and soul of work, family and community. As a system it is devoid of morality and unimpressed with social values. Money is the motive force. These are historic facts. Denunciation is as pointless as celebration. We live inside the capitalist system and cannot escape its consequences.

While acknowledging the pain and destruction caused by the operations of capitalist economy, we can also embrace the possibilities it allows. When an economy operates without particular reference to family, faith, gender and location, it admits the dream of freedom. When traditional lifeways are destroyed, there is a gap where gender fluidity and chosen family become imaginable. The possibilities we develop in queer lives and identities point to these nascent tendencies inside the capitalist system – tendencies that can never be realized without radical social change. The queer nation is multicultural and multinational. We hold the whole world in our minds and hearts, even as we suffer the material consequences of globalization and fight against the global hegemony of industrial society. Individual autonomy, chosen family, gender parity and global equality are always-broken promises inside the capitalist system. And right at the heart of contemporary economic practices, homosexuality unfolds as a space in which these promises are pledged.

Others refuse the broken promises inside the capitalist system by embracing beliefs antagonistic to its tendencies – ethnic nationalism, religious fundamentalism, violent homophobia. Such beliefs are nonsensical. They have no material basis. They cannot be challenged or modified by experience. But obvious inauthenticity does not weaken these modes of "thought." On the contrary, it is an essential part of the charm. Ethnic nationalists, religious fundamentalists and violent homophobes can transcend history and analysis with passion and certainty. They can make a community with a strong sense of belonging simply by hating what they are not. Our murder is at the heart of their identity with one another.[3]

Queer people are called to an opposite form of community. Instead of a sense of belonging that begins in hatred, ours begins in love. Our community is open instead of closed, healing instead of murderous, freely chosen instead of compulsory, broad and free-wheeling instead of narrow and restricted. Community nurtures us as we build it.

This precious community is just what the democrats would refuse us. Democrats claim to accept the material conditions and social tendencies of capitalism. Yet they deny the great collective forms of being that bring hope to history and give shape to all our lives. They imagine a social body composed of free individuals. Queer people become, in this view, no more than individuals who engage in a variety of queer behaviors, and who otherwise are the same as everyone else. Our private life doesn't matter, the democrats say. Whether we are homosexual or not is of no importance to them. They don't need to hear about it or see it celebrated in the streets.

In certain unattainable conditions, like the absence of homophobia, it may be possible to see ourselves as individuals who are – almost – no different. It is a way to deny our power and erase our threat. Our collective identity as queer people is what lets us witness and practice the possible future inside the present tense. Individual freedom, global consciousness, gender fluidity and chosen family do not exist and cannot come into being without us. Queer community is shaped by history and the economic conditions of contemporary industrial society, yet we are prescient and opposite. Without our cultural identity and sense of belonging, our difference is annihilated. We become what the democrats would have us be – serial individuals, producers, consumers – content to run the machines and eat the unripe fruits of free wage labour. If queer is not the crux of who we are, then we pose no alternative, assert no ideal, and imagine no different world than this.

Democrats want to imagine community as an aggregate of free individuals, as if the inequality and violence of capitalism could be magically transcended. This community will always stay abstract and unattainable – a community that cannot write the songs or empty the bedpans. Our collective identity as queer people is a dynamic alternative. We can accept both singularity and plurality as historically constituted facts. We know our solitude and uniqueness as both a "well of loneliness" and a precious gift. We suffer our collective identity, and it gives us wings.

We cannot step outside the pain of the present into a utopian space where the dream of individual freedom and nourishing community comes true. But we can grasp and craft the possible future that stands opposite inside the present. Being queer, we choose and practice the modes of thought and ways of life that are at once enabled and suppressed by the capitalist system. We are the future that always emerges, only to be distorted and pushed back, by contemporary industrial society. On the way to this possible future, homosexuality is both pathway and vision. Collectively and individually we create a radical new meaning for the world.

Khnumhotep and Niankhkhnum were ancient Egyptian royal servants during the Fifth Dynasty of Egyptian pharaohs, c. 2400 BCE. They were buried together and are listed as "royal confidants" in their joint tomb.

Family

The homophobes always claim, "homosexuality undermines the family." But nothing is harder on the family than heterosexuality, at least as it is engaged within the tiny parameters of the single family dwelling. Driven by the legal fiction of paternity, or the requirements of capitalism for free wage labour, modern life tends to separate heterosexual couples and their offspring from large communities and extended families. The post-war dream of suburban living takes people even farther from friends and kin. Inside the house in the suburbs, central heating, convenience food, and gender-marked spaces further separate men, women and children from each other. Older patterns of communal living disappear.[1]

The phrase "nuclear family" comes into the language in 1947, two years after the first nuclear bombs were detonated. The metaphor describes the situation pretty well: families structured like atoms, discrete entities, with a father and mother at the nucleus, and children who revolve around them. Add to this the fact that science and society have managed to split the atomic nucleus, creating a violent explosion from the chain reaction, fission leading to further fission. Inside this unstable and dangerous construct, who would not be lonely, angry and afraid?

Homosexuals escape this fate. We are the women who can say to their mothers, with Audre Lorde:

> But I have peeled away your anger
> down to the core of love
> and look mother
> I am
> a dark temple where your true spirit rises
> beautiful
> and tough as chestnut[2]

We are the men who, as in Ranier Maria Rilke's poem, stand up during supper and walk outdoors, while "another man, who remains inside/ his own house,/ dies there, inside the dishes and the glasses. . . ."[3] In each queer person there is a true spirit that cannot shine in the dead forms and obligatory gestures of nuclear family life. We peel away the anger, down to the core of love. It gives us a different chance at living.

Being queer means we do not let mother and father alone create us. We are nurtured by the world, taught to live by one another. As children we look outside the family for mentors and teachers who can show us other ways of living. Our kinship is not just with the family tree of heterosexual pairings, even including the odd spinster aunt and bachelor uncle whose branch is truncated. Our ancestors include real trees – madrone, oak – and flowers: pansy, narcissus, hyacinth. We claim kinship with salmon swimming upstream, transgendered grizzly bears that copulate and give birth through their penises, homosexual male black swans and their beloved offspring, lesbian spinner dolphins who fuck each other while they swim.[4] We have an affinity with other societies, where nuclear families are unknown. In the words of archetypal psychologist James Hillman, "ancestors are not bound to human bodies and certainly not confined to human souls."[5]

"Honor thy father and thy mother." Hillman points out that "the Fifth Commandment, along with the ones preceding it, aims to eliminate all traces of pagan polytheism. . . ." For polytheism a larger view of ancestry, and our kinship with all life, is an informing vision. Queer harkens back to the idolatry of the old nature religions.

Henri Toulouse-Lautrec (1864-1901). *Two Girlfriends.* Wikimedia.

Called outside the nuclear family to find our origins, we are freed of what Hillman calls the "parental fallacy." Mothers and fathers are not the primary instruments of our fate. We can attend to the social, environmental, and economic forces that shape us. We can leave behind infantile deprivations, without harboring the resentments that seem to stunt so many lives. Sometimes, we can even embrace people in our family of origin. It seems easier to forgive them for not being the abstract fantasy family we might have dreamed of, when we are not trying to reproduce the thing ourselves.

"We are family," as the song goes. In queer community, we have what the homophobes promoting "family values" yearn for. While they look to constitute family by enforcing gender inequalities, promoting guilt, and compelling dependencies, the children pay. In Canada and the United States, more children and adolescents die from suicide than from cancer, AIDS, birth defects, influenza, heart disease and pneumonia combined.[6] Modeling alternate forms of love and belonging, advocating for the rights of children, and creating alternate spaces of support for escapees from the nuclear family blast, we do undermine the family.

John D'Emilio writes, "building an 'affectional community' .... we may prefigure the shape of personal relationships in a society grounded in equality and justice rather than exploitation and oppression, a society where autonomy and security do not preclude each other, but coexist."[7] For the sake of young people trapped in hopeless isolation and abject dependency, the end of the nuclear family cannot come soon enough.

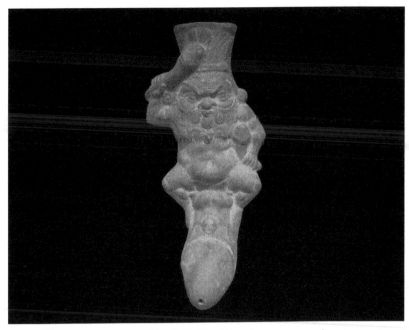

Rhyton representing an ithyphallic Bes. Painted terra cotta, ptolemaic era.
Photo: Rama. Wikimedia

Darkness

"People invent categories in order to feel safe. White
people invented black people to give white people identity. . . . Straight cats invented faggots so they could sleep
with them without becoming faggots themselves."

– James Baldwin to Nikki Giovanni[1]

Wait until dark. After nightfall, in the shadows, under the earth, at
the bottom of the river, before the beginning and after the end of life,
darkness waits for us. Sweet, secret, fearful, fecund: the dark holds
and hides us. The vampire wakes. The carnival begins. The thief dons a
mask. Dreams envelope us in unacknowledged urgencies.

Darkness is the time and space of homosexuality. Queers play in the shadowy, secret spaces inside and outside ordinary life. Homosexuality is disowned, repressed, forgotten, denied – and visited surreptitiously after dark. Heterosexuality is posed as the benign norm, the majority choice – a sexuality of bright-lit rooms and conscious knowing. Normal, ordinary, unmarked, unremarkable – heterosexuality is a name for closing in around emptiness. It was not always so. Historian Jonathan Katz finds that the term "heterosexual" was first used to describe a pervert – someone hypersexual and bent on pleasure, instead of reproduction. The contemporary meaning of "heterosexual" evolved through the late 19th and early 20th century. First homosexuality assumed its present meaning, and homosexuals became a described and reviled minority. Then heterosexuality was posed as a term for homosexuality's opposite – the unstudied, unmarked majority. Katz shows how heterosexuality comes to mean an unquestioned norm and unscrutinized posture with power-over and difference-from homosexuality in an historically specific system of superior and inferior pleasures. The concept of heterosexuality has no meaning and no power without the looming specter of homosexuality.

Through the concept of heterosexuality, opposite-sex eroticism is drained of darkness, deprived of the capacity for sin and transgression. When men and women clutch each other, they understand their passions as normal, natural and inevitable. Perverts are other people – anyone who looks outside the limits. Heterosexuality is an identity that consigns the nightmare and the Beast to an other, or to an inner darkness harboured with dread and yearning.

Whiteness also names a normative space. White racial identity only has meaning in power-over and difference-from non-whiteness. David Roediger describes whiteness as "the empty and terrifying attempt to build an identity on what one isn't and on whom one can hold back."[2] Whiteness also took its present shape in the 19th century, when race was bedecked with the new evolutionary science, and posed as an immutable fact instead of a violent and volatile regime. Whiteness invented a phanstasmagoric unity between the warring peoples and classes of Europe – at least in North America – while Europe was torn to pieces with class conflicts and inter-national warfare. Identifying with whiteness conferred enormous privilege. The wages of whiteness included property, food, mobility, suffrage, access to medical treatment, the right to territory. The obvious material benefits were supplemented by "a public and psychological wage," W.E.B. DuBois pointed out in 1914.[3] The price of the ticket was forgetting or denying darkness and becoming white. The complexities and divisions that make up anyone's identity got closed down to this: are you light enough to pass as white, or not?

Historical and economic roots nourish the culture and psychology of whiteness. Whiteness is white bread and process cheese, vanilla sex, the absence of suffering, the sound of silence. It is a culture Roediger describes as "the absence of culture." It is a psychology of empty minds and pitiless hearts. Amnesia, denial and evasion are constituent elements of whiteness. Like heterosexuality, whiteness is constructed by the disavowal of darkness. Blood, earth, sin and shadow are ascribed to racialized others. James Baldwin comments, "The white man's unadmitted – and apparently, to him, unspeakable – private fears and longings are projected onto the Negro."[4] Whiteness belongs to daylight hours, well-lit streets and conscious knowing. Chaos, compulsion, the nightmare and the Beast are consigned to an other, or to the inner darkness that is white racial identity's unacknowledged burden.

Baldwin urges white people to meet and embrace their inner darkness, if they would be released from its tyranny. "The only way [the white man] can be released from the Negro's tyrannical power over him is to consent, in effect, to become black himself, to become a part of that suffering and dancing country that he now watches wistfully from the heights of his lonely powers and … visits surreptitiously after dark." Baldwin calls us to admit the refused shadows and integrate the Beast that whiteness projects onto an other.

The material relations of racism implicate white people in guilt and shame. But whiteness is constituted by the denial of guilt and the repudiation of shame. Pretense, disavowal and forgetting create the privileged space of white racial identity. So white-identified people are singularly unprepared to confront reality, and to change it.

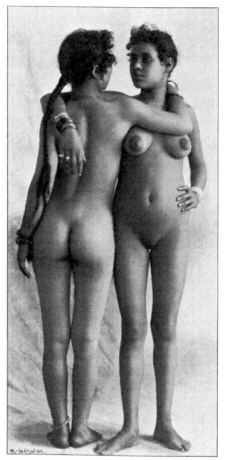

A. Schuler. 1904. Two 16 year old mulatto from Cairo.

Whiteness and heterosexuality, with their refused shadows and dearth of darkness, are entwined identities and modes of being. Queer lives could be "sites of resistance to the reproduction of racism" (Ruth Frankenberg).[5] But the ideologies of sex and race circumscribe the positions from which we act and infect the images in which we dream. We claim homosexuality is normal and ordinary, instead of allowing our boundless perversity. We pursue the right to marry, instead of a broad vision of social and economic change. Being included in the existing culture – television! – is valued over making a new culture that honors the precious, distinctive and radically transforming aspects of our lives. Homosexuality is whitewashed. Racism is tolerated in queer communities. Gay identity has little appeal for many homosexually-active, non-white men and women.

Queer people who identify as white, without critiquing whiteness, are bound to retreat from each possibility and promise that being queer contains. Whiteness cannot be transcended by paying lip service to multiculturalism. We must take responsibility for white racial identity, and fight it at each place it enters our discourse and our dreams. Homosexuality can be one way to dismantle whiteness. We can use our capacities for transgression to imagine radical alternatives and create new worlds. We can forgo our claim to power in favor of a passion for justice. Instead of projecting our own darkness onto others, or onto marginalized aspects of the queer community, we can reclaim the disowned self and "become black." We undermine the psychic space of both whiteness and heterosexuality when we eschew normalcy, and love the darkest aspects of self and world, world and self.

Two women, perhaps Demeter and Persephone, circa 100 BC, terracotta, Myrina. British Museum Department of Greek & Roman Antiquities: room 22

The Mother and The Maid

"I dream of a place between your breasts
to build my house like a haven
where I plant my crops
in your body
an endless harvest
where the commonest rock
is moonstone and ebony opal
giving milk to all my hungers
and your night comes down upon me
like a nurturing rain."

– AUDRE LORDE[1]

The Mother and the Maid appear as a dyad over and over in the myths and stories of the West. Sometimes they are one woman, like the Virgin / Mother of Christianity. Sometimes they are a lesbian couple, like the Two Goddesses at the most famous sanctuary in ancient Greece, Eleusis· Demeter and Kore; Earth Mother and Maid.

The story goes like this: the two inseparable goddesses are split apart when the Virgin Kore is abducted by Hades, Lord of the Dead. Demeter grieves inconsolably. She rages so violently that every seed is prevented from sprouting. The earth is barren, parched and withered. Finally Hades is convinced to release the ravished Kore, so that the Earth can bloom again. At the last moment, Kore eats a pomegranate seed that Hades offers. Contaminated, she must return again every winter to spend part of the year in the land of the Dead. Every winter, Demeter grieves; the earth shrivels and dies. When the Maid returns to the Mother each spring, the whole world rejoices.

The Mother, Demeter, is Kore's mother. And she is Kore's lover. Scholar Walter F. Otto compares the relations of other daughters of Greek myths to their divine parents, and finds none so intimate. Carl Kerényi comments, "The fervor of their love for one another reminds us rather of divine lovers such as Aphrodite and Adonis. . . ."[2] If we accept that the Mother and the Maid read as lovers, we find the key to Demeter's wild grief, and Kore's withholding. The two women are bound together as closely as lovers, and separated as painfully. Reunited, they fall on each other with passionate kisses.

Every lesbian relationship engages the archetype of the Maid and the Mother. This is not to say that there ever is a lesbian relationship where one partner plays the mother and the other partner plays at being mothered. But as usual, this stereotype opens into something more interesting. The turn to a woman's body is often experienced by lesbians with a sense of homecoming. Between our lover's thighs, we come home to the Mother's body. Inside her, we find a place that held us before we were born. Here we can at last become the daughters we are and give birth to.

Patriarchal culture separates mothers from daughters. It keeps women apart from one another. The social and symbolic order precludes each woman's joy, imprisons her capacities, and excises her sex. Loving lesbians, we come home to our own bodies. Reaching out to her, we touch ourselves. In the words and gestures that love invents between us, we redeem the Mother who had no power to teach us. When the Mother is delivered from her patriarchal imprisonment, we can inhabit our own bodies for the first time.

The story of the Maid and the Mother represents same-sex love as an initiation to the wild order of life and death, the deepest of Earth's mysteries. Carl Jung describes the mother archetype: "mother love...is... the mysterious root of all growth and change; the love that means homecoming, shelter, and the long silence from which everything begins and in which everything ends. Intimately known and strange like Nature, lovingly tender and yet cruel like fate, joyous and untiring giver of life – mater dolorosa and mute implacable portal that closes upon the dead."[3] Demeter is Earth Mother, origin and end. It is she who speaks for (initiates) the cycle of death and rebirth in which every life is enmeshed. And it is she who grieves inconsolably, raging, refusing ever to accept or understand the loss of her beloved to Death.

Carl Kerényi interprets Kore as representing "that which constitutes the structure of the living creature apart from this endlessly repeated drama [symbolized by Demeter] of coming-to-be and passing-away, namely the uniqueness of the individual and its enthrallment to non-being."[4] That which is unique in us will die. It is our individuality which differentiates us each from the continuum of being and links us with non-being and death. Kore's story invokes our inevitable fate. But where the Mother grieves and rages, the Maid surrenders. Kore accepts the initiation and moves to live inside the mystery: death in life, life in death.

We cannot have life without death, but only a shriveled semblance of life, parched by withholding. We cannot love without loss. There is no inconsolable heartbreak without unspeakable gladness. So much of contemporary society seems intent upon avoiding risk. Old age is approached as a disease to cure. Science intends to conquer disability.

Children are confined to playpens. Love appears only as weak senti-ment. We need the Maid and the Mother to guide us to the mystery, or we will stay stuck on the surface, clinging to youth, picking flowers, avoiding the dark chasm where we meet loss, and grief, and mortal destiny.

Lesbian love brings us home to the Mother we never had. Through our lovers we find our source and our surcease. We experience enmesh-ment with one another and with the continuum of all life. And yet lesbian love challenges us to differentiation. We are enjoined in battle against the patriarchy, wounded, denied, called to use every ounce of our power. Our lovers cherish our strengths. They summon us to our capacities. They admire our songs. As personal voice and individuality grows stronger, the threat and risk of loss is greater. Our passions lead us to the maw of fear. If we dare to move inside, we face the season of despair. And we come, again and again, to Spring.

Through union with the Mother we experience the unity of life. Through identity with the Maid, we come to know our uniqueness, solitude and strength. Patriarchal socialization requires each of us to disavow the Mother and break irrevocably with the unity of self and world we know in her body. [5] Individuality is valued and com-monality is denied. The end of life is as feared as the beginning. The Maid and the Mother invite us to a different way of being in the world, extending and transforming the empathic continuum of life with each person's individuality and differentiation.

The mystery accepts that, always, some part of world or self is lost and broken. We can admit grief, without being paralyzed by fear of grief. We can go down beneath the surface and live with our own deepest fears, until love bids us back to a beginning. When we meet her again, the sun is shining. Birds sing. Flowers begin to open. The air smells of fresh spring rain. Our joy in each other's arms is boundless. Our love goes deep enough to call the world to life.

Ary Scheffer, 1795-1858 (artist); L. Prang & Co. (publisher). *Christ and St. John.*
1861-1897 (approximate). Chromolithograph; Boston Public Library, Print Department

The Tree God

Among mentally ill people in contemporary North America, there
are two common delusions. In a manic manifestation of their illness,
schizophrenics often claim to be Jesus – though no one else can recognize it. Alternatively, patients in a depressed or paranoid phase of
mental illness often imagine that everyone thinks they are homosexual. "Jesus" and "the homosexual" are cultural symbols that fit together,
like two sides of one coin: best/worst, powerful/powerless, exalted/de-
spised. At root Jesus and the homosexual only make sense as a single
entity. They are the contemporary faces of an ancient myth: the divine
child, born of the Virgin / Mother. Jesus and the homosexual are two
aspects of a vegetation god who rises unalterably from the earth, only
to be torn apart and devoured when the time comes. This god of green

and growing things is an archetype that appears around the world, throughout time, in a multitude of myths, stories and cultural practices. Madness can be a key to the mythic dimensions of any culture. In this culture, it often points to the Tree God: Jesus/the homosexual.

Like the homosexual, Jesus is born miraculously in a most unlikely place. As a child he is exposed to threat and persecution, solitude and loneliness. Jung writes of this archetype, "The 'child' is all that is abandoned and exposed and at the same time, divinely powerful; the insignificant, dubious beginning, and the triumphal end."[1] The mortal god leads a recognizably queer life. Jesus leaves home too late or too soon, gathers a band of lovers, performs miracles. He is crucified by the reigning powers and loved by a loyal underground. Betrayed and abandoned, tortured, murdered, his death is the sacrifice that brings the resurrection and the life. The meaning of his slaughter is the resurrection. His energy is life itself, and cannot be contained. Like the homosexual, he dies, he is murdered. And he continues despite his enemies. Miraculously born again and again, in the face of every punishment and prohibition, the homosexual persists.

"Cleave a piece of wood," says Jesus in the Gospel of Thomas. "I am there."[2] Jesus is the tree-god, as we can be: rooted, branching, infinitely expressive. We soar – "'scuze me while I kiss the sky" – and we go dark and deep, drawing nourishment from the underground. The tree is a sign for one, the unique and lonely individual, but underground its roots entwine with other trees, with earth and worms, and with the cyclic unity of life and death that is our world unfolding.

From the Taoist mountain spirit Shan Gui, through the Ancient Greek Dionysus and the Navaho Begochidi, vegetation gods around the world are androgynous. They have in common with Jesus and the homosexual a conjoining of masculine and feminine qualities, a hermaphrodism of body and soul. The androgyne symbolizes wholeness in a gender-bifurcated society, pointing to a possible future – psychic and social – and evoking a mythological past. Jung comments, "Notwithstanding its monstrosity, the hermaphrodite has gradually turned into a subduer of conflicts and a bringer of healing, and it acquired this meaning in relatively early phases of civilization."[3]

The conjoining of male and female attributes does seem monstrous in a culture based on gender difference and an economy fueled by the unpaid work of women. Is it despite or because of this monstrosity that the hermaphrodite is healer? Christ, like the homosexual, is both the phallus and the wound. Uniting these opposites in a single body, the Tree God takes us deep into the labyrinth of unconscious processes. The Minotaur demands its tribute, and the hermaphrodite also requires a sacrifice. When we embrace the monster and open its gifts, we sacrifice all the self-certainty and social approbation that gender identity affords. If we have hitherto been women, we pick up the phallus. If we have hitherto been men, we experience the wound. We become monstrous – fabulous, horrible – to everyone who stays outside the labyrinth, stuck on one or another side of gender difference. Yet here we are – a beacon of hope, a symbol of wholeness, a reminder of the repressed or forgotten moment of splitting into extremes with opposite characteristics.

The conscious mind is always limited, narrow in scope, constrained by personal history and social mores. If we are also the indefinite extent of our unconscious processes, we are stronger and weaker, bigger and smaller, older and younger than consciousness. Such wholeness cannot be claimed by fiat nor won through achievement. It can only be glimpsed and guessed at, lost and found, by exploring archetypes and attending to dreams.

The Tree God – as a symbol that is at once male and female, mortal and immortal, powerful and vulnerable – carries us deep into the earth and high into the sky. He is a way in, a path through, and the monster at the centre of the labyrinth. Joyous and suffering, exalted and despised, he reminds us to accept paradox and eschew resolution. As the contemporary representations of this ancient archetype, queer people suffer the scapegoating, and we carry the possibility of healing. With our miraculous persistence and our infinite complexity, we are a kind of catechism. Holding opposites without seeking compromise or the cheap solution of indifference, we pose a way to wash the world of sin.

Antonio da Correggio (c. 1531–1532), *Ganymede Abducted by the Eagle*, Oil on canvas, 163.5 cm × 70.5 cm (64.4 in × 27.8 in), Kunsthistorisches Museum. Wikimedia.

Air

Gay is gaiety. We laugh and clown; humor is a subversive tool and a way of walking through the world. Frivolity and lightness is air – joy, our natural element.

We are at home in air, as flying spirits, winged beasts and stars. Angels, fairies and witches are all patterns of queer identity, different ways that we have wings. Air is Eros, the winged, androgynous daemon described by Plato as "the craving and pursuit of wholeness."[1] Through Eros we seek our original form. In ourselves and each other we find our double, our twin, the wholeness described by the archetype of Innocence.

Air is the Sky God of Christian tradition, devoid of earth and instinct, the god that James Baldwin calls "a profound and dangerous failure of concept." And yet this god is used to condemn "an incalculable number of humans to something less than life."[2]

Air is without body, weight and gravity. Nevertheless, the atmosphere sustains us. Breath is life. Effeminacy is airy light, and yet it makes us possible. The effeminate soul, transformed in receptivity and sustained in artificiality, is the virgin mother of invention.

Air is annunciation, the language that conceives us, the silence through which we disappear. We soar in air, when we use words, laughter, love and community to lend each other wings.

Human swastika motif from a Pictish recumbent grave-slab, at Meigle Museum, Perthshire, 7th century. Photographer: CM Dixon

Laughter

"Energy is eternal delight."

– WILLIAM BLAKE[1]

Being gay is linked with laughter, etymologically and ontologically. Gay, from the Old French *gai*, means we are full of merriment, bright in appearance, and loose in our ways of living. We are called fools and we are called to be fools – outrageous in our joy and exuberant in our laughter. We partake of the carnival, the magic place where all is permitted, the time when opposites combine and hierarchies briefly collapse. The way of the Fool is to embrace the carnival's magic and bring its insights to lighten the everyday. Because we live in bright costumes, free of conventions, we can see and say when the emperor has no clothes.

Fools can say what others are afraid to say, or cannot even see, because Fools laugh at social convention. Freedom makes them wise; humor makes them palatable. Laughter opens the heart and evokes the animating spirit. If we are Fool enough, then queer becomes, as Andrew Hodges and David Hutter put it, a means of "recognize[ing] the stupidity that lies at the heart of every cliché judgment and delighting in its exuberant reversal."[2]

A Fool in the tarot deck appears as a Joker in an ordinary card deck – a wild card that can be high or low. Players are thrilled when they pick it up; they dread being stuck with it. We too are wild cards, shape-shifters moving in and out of closets, changing costumes, assuming secret identities. We each in our own way bear witness to the remarkable transformations and reinventions through which homosexuality appears and disappears, throughout history, in every corner of the world. There is no queer "identity" inasmuch as identity means "sameness." We are mutable and multiple. We are everywhere and nowhere. Hypervisible in exuberant carnivals of gay pride, and invisible in seamless coherence with every human community, homosexuality suggests not identity but diversity.

Diversity strengthens us individually as it does collectively. A homosexual cannot have only a single, unitary Self. Survival depends upon having diverse selves. We are called to use our capacity for magic and transformation. Sometimes we play dead, or crawl under rocks. Like a Winnebago Trickster we might become someone of the opposite sex; we might marry and bear children. When we are discovered, we escape and flee towards a new adventure, exhilarated. The secret of reincarnation is embodied in the metamorphoses of each queer life.

Where others craft a life out of concern for comfort and convention, being queer means we are released from this fate. We embrace danger when we mock convention and cast doubt on accepted behaviors. Homosexuality is shocking. To assume its hazards we need a relaxed spirit, with an ebullient sense of lust and freedom. We learn to trust not in any predictable outcomes, but in our own resilience.[3] Madeline McMurray writes, "An over-structured personality has little opportunity to participate in the dance of life, while the personality of the fool turns many a joyous cartwheel."[4]

The Trickster is a clownish figure in the myths of many cultures who breaks the rules, plays malicious pranks, and is exposed by excess appetites to all sorts of tortures. Trickster stories seem to invariably include dirty jokes about gender-bending and homoeroticism, just as stories about gender-bending and homoeroticism involve trickery and evoke hilarity. A Coast Salish story tells of an old grandmother who pretends to die. Then she pulls back her wrinkled skin, puts a hammer between her legs, and goes home to bed both of her granddaughters. When the granddaughters' sore vulvas lead them to discover that their new husband is really their old grandmother, they tickle her to death.[5] Navaho, Lakota, Crow and Apache tell stories of Coyote, who transforms himself into a woman so he can seduce a handsome man. But when Coyote gives birth to twin coyote-infants, his true identity is revealed.[6] At Pakistani weddings a young woman dresses as an old man. As he dances with a girl, or embraces the bride's mother, the other women mock his virility.[7]

Carl Jung comments that people lose track of their capacity for introspection and independent action in a society that fails to honor the Trickster. He writes, "The so-called civilized man has forgotten the trickster. . . . He never suspects that his own hidden and apparently harmless shadow has qualities whose dangerousness exceeds his wildest dreams. As soon as people get together in masses and submerge the individual, the shadow is mobilized, and, as history shows, may even be personified and incarnated."[8] We live in a humourless culture that projects and elects its shadows. Homophobia is interwoven with this process. In 2001 when this chapter was written, the right-wing rulers of the United States were elected on an explicitly homophobic platform. Homosexuality is their projected shadow, while they become the elected shadow ready to inflict a brutal regime upon the world. In the spring of 2003, they moved against international law and world public opinion to wage war on Iraq. Homophobia served as a vital weapon. Saddam Hussein and the Iraqi people were "homosexualized" by U.S. troops, whose battle preparations inevitably include such motivating chants as "Faggot, faggot, down the street. Shoot him, shoot him, till he retreats."[9] In the lead-up to the war, Washington criticized UN weapons inspector Hans Blix for being "soft" on Saddam Hussein, while rumours that he was homosexual were circulated in the Middle East and America. Another UN weapons inspector was reviled for his involvement with a pansexual S&M group. When the French failed to support the U.S. invasion of Iraq, they were called effeminate pansies. During the occupation of Iraq, Americans at Abu Gharib prison tortured Iraqi prisoners by sodomizing them and forcing them to simulate sex acts with one another. Homophobia was just as rampant on the Iraqi side. The year before the war, Saddam Hussein joined Arab counterparts (including U.S. ally Saudi Arabia) by enacting laws punishing homosexuality with death. It was billed as a gesture against "Western" cultural values – albeit homosexuality had previously been unlegislated in secular Iraq, while it was illegal in many U.S. states. Homophobia thrives in conditions where individuals are deprived of their capacities for introspection and independent action – in societies that fail to listen to Fools, honor Tricksters, and use the insight humour allows. People can become dangerous and violent more easily when they stop laughing at themselves.

Trickster, Clown, and Fool – these images are powerful, shaping presences in the lives of queer people, and in the stereotypes that oppress us. Through them we can embrace the world with audacity and courage. We can hone our capacities for disguise and metamorphosis. We can love each other with lasciviousness and joy. These patterns of experience flow from a fundamentally different world-view than that espoused in the global marketplace. If we can be Fools – choosing laughter and risk over comfort and security – then greed and self-aggrandizement cannot be the motive power of all life.

Frank Meadow Sutcliffe (1853-1941). *Three Naked Boys Around a Coble*, 1880s.
The Bridgeman Art Library, Object 407008.

Innocence

The Dogon of Africa believe that every child is born with both a male and a female soul. At puberty, one soul is chosen and the other is cut away with cliterodectomy or circumcision. Without this violent excision, no one would develop the inclination for procreation.

The Androgyne is a symbol of wholeness, an original innocence from which we are wrenched away by the requirements of gender, culture and maturity. In Western culture, at least, learning the requirements of sexuality is equivalent to the paring away of capacities. Boys forgo sensitivity, receptivity and inwardness to assume the perks of manhood. Girls learn to denigrate and fear their power and independence to become acceptable women. These psychic excisions are violent and painful mutilations. Often the wounds refuse to heal.

Queers are called away from the carnage, back to the carefree joys of an ideal childhood. Like Peter Pan, we say "I won't grow up," and it gives us wings. We refuse the weight and obligations of so-called maturity. With irritating acumen, people keep calling us "boys" and "girls" no matter how old we become. So long as we avoid the tasks and wounds of adult male and female sexual identities, we are identified with the archetype of innocence.

Mark Thompson writes, "I would define gay people as possessing a luminous quality of being, a differentness that accentuates the gifts of compassion, empathy, healing, interpretation and enabling. I see gay people as in-between-ones; uniting opposing forces as one." Ostensibly opposing forces organize thought as they organize life. Masculine / feminine is one such duality. Bound together like a pair of mules headed in opposite directions, male / female is going nowhere and getting exhausted. Queer people slip between binaries, building bridges or creating strategies of resistance. Thompson continues, "For me, gay people represent the archetype of innocence, a shaman's tool that allows access to a more primal world, one where his / her work is done."[1] With this notion of innocence as a "shaman's tool," Thompson suggests a way through another ostensible opposition – that between initiation and innocence. Queer innocence is not constituted in denial, withholding, and fear of life experience. It is a way of meeting inner and outer worlds with optimism and trust – opening like a flower, bending towards the light, responding to the inner impulse.

At the movies, on the street, in the news, and in the popular imagination, homosexuality is linked with crime and violence. Priests rape altar boys. A lesbian becomes a serial killer. In Littleton, Colorado, young boys called "faggots" murder fourteen classmates, then themselves. These characters may have nothing to do with the great adventure of being gay, but they have much to do with the presence of homosexuality in the general culture. Occasionally homosexuality is not so obviously an aspect of the crime or the criminal, but it is always an aspect of the punishment. Every cop show, news report, and sociological study restates the threat, usually without quite saying the words – no one gets out of prison without some kind of (unwanted) homosexual experience.

We may be tempted to counter all this association of homosexuality with crime and violence by self-righteously proclaiming our innocence. Donning a public mask of wide-eyed innocence is nothing like using innocence as a "shaman's tool." As a mask and a posture, innocence invites wounding and mortification. We talk about the effeminate boy, born gay, bullied into suicide. We talk about the lesbian mother, who realizes her true self, only to lose custody of her beloved children. Innocence segues into pain and loss, inviting pity, beseeching forgiveness. If we are guilty of being gay, it's not our fault. Blame genetics, blame mom and dad, blame the society that oppresses us. They can accept us – or perhaps more to the point, we can accept ourselves, when we are innocent and therefore victims.

Embracing the adventure of homosexuality, we can lift this mask of innocence. Cruelty, aggression, promiscuity and violence can surely be acknowledged without subsuming our souls. Depravity claims space. It can occupy us as the polar opposite of false innocence, expressed in pathologies and exorcised with self-righteousness. Or depravity can find subtle expressions and finally-articulated niches, in costume, erotic play, art, philosophy, sexual cultures. "The inner world is a place of blood and fire, tears and mud," Mark Thompson writes elsewhere.[2] Our worst nightmares lead us deep inside. Given time and attention, they feed culture and nourish the soul.

We include both wide-eyed innocence and genuine depravity. Accepting this, we can use innocence as a "shaman's tool," instead of a brittle mask. We can honor the polymorphous perversity that curiously belongs to the deepest innocence. Deepening our innocence with initiation, we learn to invite pleasure over mortification. Purity of heart, playfulness, trust and openness are pathways to defilement, self-acceptance, and integration of the Shadow.

Eros is a child like this: androgynous, pre-pubescent, mischievous. The mingling of Eros and Chaos begins the world. Certainly, Eros and Chaos create us. Often with surprising reversals and a chaotic re-ordering of values and expectations, love invents queer lives. We are perverted by desire – turned around and connected with a primal order, a cosmogonic energy.

Our love for one another can be profoundly innocent – playful, open-hearted, trusting. It can be limitless, passionate, and chaotic. In one another's arms, we hold an awful mystery, a terrible pain, an incomprehensible depravity. And we hold on. Following the innocent heart of desire, we learn to love each other whole.

We-Wa, a Zuni berdache, weaving , photo by John K. Hillers, 1843-1925, Photographer
(NARA record: 3028457) - U.S. National Archives and Records Administration.
Licensed under Public Domain via Wikimedia Commons.

Effeminacy

Anal rape is fundamental to relations between men. From antiquity
to the present, adolescent gangs have used the threat and fact of anal
rape to construct and maintain male hierarchies. In Crete c. 400 BC,
young men abducted and raped younger boys who then served them as
"wives" until they reached the appropriate age for marriage to women.
Historian Richard Trexler writes, "It has long been a truism that the
family is the foundation of the state, but . . . . those relations between
males that begin in gangs and continue in these first homosexual mar-
riages already provide a foundation for the state – that is, that set of relations between males that peaks in the power of the male sovereign."[1]

Proving the power of one man while subordinating and shaming another, anal rape can be seen as more fundamental to patriarchal social organization than any different-sex interaction.

Anal rape is an effective expression of power and weapon of terror in part because of prohibitions on anal eroticism. These prohibitions have deep historical roots in western culture. Same-sex passions were an expected part of life for men and boys in Ancient Greece, but intercrucal (between the thighs) intercourse was the prescribed practice. Anal sex, and in particular anyone who took the receptive role in anal intercourse, was viewed with deep suspicion. During the Roman Empire, anal sex was viewed as permissible within strict limits. Roman men could anally penetrate lower class men and boys, but citizens (upper-class, adult men) could not themselves be penetrated. Penetration effeminates. Being a man means always being on top.

Leo Bersani notes that the prohibitions on anal intercourse reveal sex outside its mystifications. Getting fucked means being effeminated, and that means being wounded, shamed, and powerless. Men cannot be fucked, unless they are (made into) women.[2] The threat of being effeminated – so fundamental to relations between men – is subverted by men who embrace effeminacy. The affectations and vulnerabilities of effeminate men pose the possible pleasures, for men, of powerlessness. Effeminacy evokes the recuperation of anal eroticism, and the corresponding penetration and violation of phallic masculinity.

Of course there is no necessary association of same-sex passion with either effeminacy or anal eroticism. Other cultures may eschew the anus as a site of pleasure and prohibition. And men who love men, far from being considered effeminate, are in some cultures held to be more manly than anyone else.[3] But in Western culture from the 19th century the homosexual is characterized, in Foucault's well-known formulation, by "a kind of interior androgyny, a hermaphrodism of the soul," and "a way of inverting the masculine and feminine in oneself.[4] No matter how macho his personal style or how tight his sphincter, every gay man, just by being gay, bears some relationship with effeminacy.

A gay man, or some part of his soul, is soft, weak and womanish
– though he is not merely debased and contemptible as a woman is
inside a patriarchal culture. He has a penis, but it is a means of pleasure
among men, instead of a weapon of power. He has a hole; he is penetrable; but this penetration, powerlessness, and wounding is desired
and desirable. Luce Irigaray writes, "when the penis itself becomes a
means of pleasure among men, the phallus loses its power."[5] When the
anus becomes a means and a site of pleasure, the power of intercourse
to effeminate becomes moot. If softness, weakness and vulnerability
can be embraced by men, if men do not always have to be on top, then
phallic masculinity becomes a joy and a toy. Relationships between
men are re-envisioned as potentially playful, erotic and free.

Fortified, tough, hard, phallic masculinity is opposite to the receptivity, flexibility, softness and inwardness indicated by anal eroticism.
Will Roscoe writes, "From the patriarchal point of view, we gay men
castrate ourselves every time we give up male privilege, every time,
especially, that we allow our bodies to be penetrated by other men. For
us, penetration is the key to ecstasy because it erases the distinction
between inside and outside. Most heterosexual men find this distinction indispensable to their sense of ego, which they tend to think of in
terms of metaphors of fortification."[6]

Freud comments on the anal eroticism of all young human beings,
noting children's interest in excretory products and functions.[7] Property too has a primary anal form. As a little boy is instructed in the
significance of his genital superiority, he learns to organize his desires
and explorations under the aegis of the phallus. Anality is repudiated;
the anus is a hole too much like the mother's. Just so, the boy's real
prick – the feeling, trembling penis – is something he is no longer
allowed to play with. The Oedipal interdict prohibits his desire, and
offers instead an insentient, indifferent identity with the Big-Prick-
In-The-Sky. The little boy's struggles against the prohibitions on his
sentient body have been described by psychoanalysis. The intended
resolution of this "complex" is that the little boy accepts these prohibitions by acknowledging the threat of castration (acknowledging sexual

difference), but assuming that he will one day possess the Big Prick of his (dead) father. This resolution is only the "ideal fiction" of mental health. More often, "success is achieved at the price of a rift in the ego which never heals but increases as time goes on" (Freud).[8] There is a licit identity-with-the-phallus, where he speaks with all the authority of phallic masculinity: insentient, closed, fortified, indifferent. And there is an illicit identity-with-castration, that cannot ever be spoken, where he still feels, trembles, wants.

Jean Broc (1771–1850), *The Death of Hyacinth*, 1801, oil on canvas, Musée Sainte-Croix

Anal eroticism harkens back to the pre-Oedipal perversity of childhood. It calls to the trembling identity-with-castration: the incoherent, forbidden, yearning and wounded self that dwells inside the guts and just under the skin. For men pinned down and pumped up by phallic masculinity, anal penetration is a radical, transforming desire. Frank Browning describes anal penetration as "an entry into the most private and sacred zones of individual identity," and "an act which shatters the authority and integrity of the male self."[9] Klaus Theweleit, writing of male fantasies, comments "Anal penetration comes to represent the opening of social prisons, admission into a hidden dungeon that guards the keys to the recuperation of the revolutionary dimension of desire. . . ."[10]

Men forgo so much when they identify with phallic masculinity. In every area of life and relationship, they are to keep things tough and dry. The Oedipal interdict would keep men devoid of care, passion and playfulness. Feeling is what characterizes the pre-Oedipal child, or the wounded body of a woman. With effeminacy, men claim a capacity for emotion, beauty and connectedness, love of home, personal sharing and adornment, an ecological concern for the web of life.[11] Instead of the indifferent, transcendent identity with the phallus, they open up to gaiety, grief and awful need.

Many lesbians reject femininity. We see that femininity is wrecked, historically, by the centuries it has functioned as a signifier of genital inferiority and of silence, submission and passivity. We leave it to effeminate men to bring alive the values that inhere in elaborate decoration, attention to surfaces, sensitivity, vulnerability and silliness. If effeminate men can hold and protect the rejected feminine, even as it endangers them to do so, they may teach us to open our own post-Oedipal bodies to risk, complication, and joy.

In the context of a prohibition on effeminacy, homoeroticism and homosexuality can coexist quite comfortably with homophobia – even, as with the Nazis, with the mass murder of gay people. It is commonplace for homosexually-active men to disavow homosexual identity, so long as they never take the receptive role in anal intercourse.[12] Anal penetration effeminates, violates, wounds and creates the effeminate soul of the homosexual. Without gay identity, when the actors do not affirm that they are homosexual, homosexuality takes place within limits that affirm and enforce power relations between men and contempt for women. Accepting or embracing queer identity means being called outside these limits. Claiming a capacity for effeminacy, for anal eroticism and the pleasures of penetration, effeminacy re-appropriates the meaning and magic of same-sex desire to its revolutionary potential.

It is a truism that avoiding anality leads to disenchantment, parsimony, and an obsessive concern with order and boundaries. Anal eroticism is a doorway to enchantment, excess and transgression. Effeminacy affirms the existence of penetrable men who forego phallic authority, and instead choose radical openness. It allows us to envision the phallus as a toy, the penis as blood and skin, and the designation of sexual difference as an ongoing alchemy that could someday become playful, poetic, and free.

Dream of Three Wise Men (Magi). Capital from Autun cathedral. Sculptor: Gislebertus, 12th century. Photo: Cancre.

Annunciation

"My friend thinks I keep silence, who am only choked
with letting it out so fast. Does he forget that new
mines of secrecy are constantly opening up in me?"

– Henry David Thoreau[1]

In January 1933 Adolph Hitler became chancellor of Germany. Homosexual rights organizations were outlawed twenty-five days later. In May that year, the Nazis held a city-wide bookburning in Berlin. Magnus Hirschfeld's Institute for Sexual Sciences was destroyed, along with his large collection of scholarly writings, case studies, and archival materials on homosexuality. Homosexuals were incarcerated in concentration camps, subjected to experiments by Nazi doctors, beaten, starved and gassed. Yet historical studies of the Third Reich rarely mention the persecution of homosexuals.

Emily Dickinson's passionate letters to her sister-in-law were expurgated by her niece before they were published. All talk of kisses and ardent longings was excised. Michelangelo's grandnephew changed the gendered pronouns of the artist's sonnets to make it appear as if they were written to women instead of to boys and men. Alternative gender roles were widespread throughout indigenous societies in North America, but anthropological records fail to mention it. King Rufus (England, 12th Century) was a flaming queen, but historians gloss over it. History, current events, social studies, art, science and sex education classes in schools fail to mention same-sex passions or homosexuality. The very existence of the GLBTQ population is burned up, cut out, covered up, ignored – with monstrous, deadly silence.

Silence = Death, as the AIDS Coalition To Unleash Power put it, when for years no action was taken to research, combat and educate people on avoiding the virus killing gay men. If we fail to rupture the silence that surrounds us, we suffocate to death. So many queer folk do not survive their teenage years. They are bullied. They are murdered. They die of suicide, drugs, alcohol and HIV. They are choked to death by silence that denies them desire, agency, history and community. So many elders die in silence. Some fail to protect their "friends" with wills and legally-executed representation agreements. They would rather lose all security and betray their life partners than be named – even posthumously – homosexual.

Suffocating silence and "the deadly elasticity of heterosexist presumption,"[2] as Eve Kofosky Sedgwick describes it, make "coming out" a continual task. Rupturing silence with an announcement of identity – with every new doctor, landlord, employee and P.T.A. meeting – is a process fraught with risk and anxiety. It takes enormous courage and has profound effects. It makes the air we breathe; it creates an environment that can sustain our lives.

We know in our bones the deadly effects of silence. Yet the silence that surrounds and suffocates queer identity also carries its gifts.

Thomas Moore calls silence an aid to enchantment. He writes, "Silence is not an absence of sound but rather a shifting of attention toward sounds that speak to the soul . . . . Silence is a positive kind of hearing which requires turning off the knob that tunes in to the active, literal life and turning on the one that amplifies the movements of the soul."[3]

Leonardo da Vinci (1452–1519). *Angel Incarnato*. 1513-1515.
Louvre Museum. Wikimedia.

In silence, without names and precedents to direct our yearnings, each one of us has to divine identity and find our life's direction by listening to the movement of our hearts. We are called to a soulful life through silence. Michel Foucault talks about the freedom silence makes possible, the multiple causes and meanings. He notes that in other cultures silence is "a specific form of experiencing a relationship with others."[4]

The silence that surrounds homosexuality makes simply "coming out" a transgression. Announcing our homosexuality, we reveal the invisible and say the unspeakable. Unannounced, queer slips back into the nether-world of secrecy and maybe-not. Queer people cannot exist without annunciation – continually repeated, judiciously withheld. Coming out always implicates those we come out to. Friends and family often feel themselves contaminated with homosexuality and concerned with defending themselves against it. Alternately, our identity can function as an opening for those who hear us, a crack in the obdurate wall of heterosexist conformity. Sometimes they can slip through to join us in a starry sky of passion and possibility.

Our mouths are sex organs when they speak the forbidden language of difference. Coming out is an erotic act. Modern life bifurcates people into visible surface and inner self.[5] Historical, cultural and economic forces wrench individuals free from predictable lifeways and social contexts where they are "known." Superficial social interactions demand more and more energy, while the "inner essence" that is each person's history, fantasy, dream and desire is constituted as a territory withheld from social life. The self is secret, and its deepest secrets are sexual secrets – libidinal drives and guilty narratives of sexual wounds and woundings. There is a yearning to be touched, seen, permitted and forgiven, and the defended territory of the "inner self" is constitutionally incapable of satisfying that yearning – at least in the superficial interactions of everyday life.

Coming out refers to this dark, secret, silent place within; it calls the "inner essence" into an act of speech. At the moment of annunciation, we give our selves away, surrendering the paranoid territory of a self that is constituted by withholding. Instead of confining our sexuality to secret sexual acts, in coming out we claim a public sexual identity. The secret is out; we make our selves the hot and slippery subject of public discourse. The air is charged with libidinal energy when we bring our selves out in social intercourse.

When we "come out," our richly productive inwardness is sublimated to social purposes. Annunciation is an act of self-disclosure that is simultaneously an act of service – a way to align the self with, and to act in the service of, the queer community. The "self" conceived in this disclosure is not individual. Transfigured by annunciation, it cannot stay self-identical. Dag Hammarskjöld, Swedish economist, Secretary General of the United Nations from 1953 until his death in 1957, international peacemaker, Nobel Prize laureate, dedicated public servant, and homosexual, writes, "…I can realize my individuality by becoming a bridge for others, a stone in the temple of righteousness."[6] Just so, coming out is a way of realizing individuality by becoming a stone, a bridge, a representative specimen.

Hammarskjöld writes of his calling, "To preserve the silence within – amid all the noise. To remain open and quiet, a moist humus in the fertile darkness where the rain falls and the grain ripens – no matter how many tramp across the parade-ground in whirling dust under an arid sky."[7] If we live, the silence surrounding queer existence can open a fertile space inside the soul. Silence can be a meditative practice and a spiritual discipline. It is a way to find the inmost images, and become nourished by the deepest wisdom. The richest veins of creativity and love can only be tapped in silence.

Queer identity is always new. Hammarskjöld writes of holding out "the chalice of our being to receive, to carry and give back. It must be held out empty – for the past must only be reflected in its polish, its shape, its capacity."[8] The past does not limit us. Language does not structure each startling movement of the heart. We are secret, silent, and in Hammarskjöld's sense, empty. We have to invent ourselves and each other. We live always new like a river: running clean, making tracks as we go. And the thick mud of the riverbed is dark and rich with forever. We have no beginning. We have no end.

Affirming and creating ourselves as queer persons with each annunciation, we can say with Hammarskjöld, "each day the first day: each day a life."

Peter Paul Rubens, *Saturn, Jupiter's father, devours one of his sons.*
1636-1638. Wikimedia.

Sky God

The first hint of same-sex sexuality in the Holy Bible appears in
Genesis 9. Ham is in his tent with his father Noah when the patriarch
is stark naked and dead drunk. Ham goes and tells his brothers, who
take a coat and, walking backwards into the tent, cover Noah. The
good brothers keep their faces averted to avoid the terrible sin of the
same-sex gaze.[1] Ham – who dared to speak of his father's nakedness,
perhaps even to laugh at the drunk old man – is condemned to be a
servant of servants, father of slaves.

The humorless god who orchestrates this absurd crime and ghastly
punishment is, as James Baldwin comments, "a profound and dangerous failure of concept."[2] This is the same god who tells Noah, "And

the fear of you and the dread of you shall be upon every beast of the earth, and upon every fowl of the air, upon all that moveth upon the earth, and upon all the fishes of the sea; into your hand are they delivered" (Genesis 9: 2). Subjugating nature, prohibiting and punishing the same-sex gaze, demanding obsequious compliance with the patriarchal order, encouraging every grotesque exploitation of stigmatized others: these strands are braided together to make a god as mean and small as they come.

The sky god of Judeo-Christian tradition hates and punishes homosexuality. Colin Spence notes that in the early days of the formation of the Hebrew nation, the Jewish people "were surrounded by cultures which celebrated male temple prostitution."[3] Hebraic injunctions against sodomy are injunctions against these eunuch priests and their magical powers. Christianity revived the notion of eunuch priests, and the Christian church wove many homoerotic images and archetypes into its iconography. But Christianity maintained and refined the Hebraic prohibition against sodomy. The humorless and punishing sky god met the needs of patriarchy and imperialism. The prohibition on sodomy kept relations between men under control – no rapture that might rupture the holy offices of trade and inheritance.

White Western Man is drained of blood and sex, earth and laughter. These are left to others and objects: women, "Negroes", natives, mother earth. The sky god represses the chthonic deities and strips homoeroticism of its power. It is a culture of denial – what Luce Irigaray calls "the sovereign authority of pretense which does not yet recognize its endogamies."[4] Goods are traded and power circulates between white men, passing from father to son – but these patriarchal relationships are purely symbolic, not erotic. There can be no pleasure without possession. False innocence is preserved by deadly violence.

Ham's brothers look the other way, and walk backwards into the tent to cover Noah's nakedness. They thereby claim a patrimony that includes the right to enslave their brother's children. Ham is a Trickster figure, the Divine Fool who laughs at the Patriarch. He tells the truth; he dares the transgression; he is alive to the possibility of sex between men and between fathers and sons. Ham's brothers will not see and cannot admit the Father's silliness or his sexuality. For them the patriarchal authority is inevitable and impenetrable. They claim a just reward for willful blindness. The sky god rewards false innocence. His subjects are preserved from inadmissible knowledge of world and self. The boundaries between Good and Evil are clear and smooth. They are policed with blame, shame and brutal violence.

The construction of race and sexuality are entwined in the story of Ham. James Baldwin suggests that the construction of the Negro and the homosexual both begin with a concept of god that "is not big enough." He writes, "To be with God is really to be involved with some enormous, overwhelming desire, and joy, and power which you cannot control, which controls you . . . . I conceive of God . . . as a means of liberation and not a means to control others."[5] Being queer, we are called to enter a gigantic imagination of god. Instead of claiming a concept of god small enough to be agreed upon, we can admit to not knowing. Not knowing is humility, emptiness, readiness. Not knowing is an open mind and a heart that can admit what is new, transforming, impossible.[6] If we don't know or understand what god is, we might prefer acceptance and love to righteousness and punishment.

To accept the horror of history, and still believe we can weave a future loving nature, honoring women, embracing homosexuality and dismantling whiteness, we need a faith past all understanding. Yet divine is there, in a sunlit moment, in the eyes of a stranger, in the arms of a lover. Despite the parsimony of the sky-god's self-appointed spokespeople, the world in all its wonder does persist.

Divine is also a verb. Being queer means walking through the world divining, with intuitive recognitions and prophetic insights. Despite the absence and denial that confronts us everywhere, we divine the love that creates us as queer people. Passion, engagement, sweet astonishment, blinding certainty – this love is an overwhelming, unpredictable power that can only be god.

Hans Baldung (1485–1545), *New Year's Greetings with Three Witches*, 1514, Pen drawing heightened with white body colour on brown prepared paper, 30.9 x 20.9 cm, Louvre Museum.

Fire

We burn with our passion for one another and we ignite forbidden desires. Fire is sexual energy: gigantic, transformative, consuming.

Fire radiates warmth and light. It makes a home, a meal, and a habitat out of a pitiless world. And fire destroys all that, in an angry instant. Cremation brings even our bones to dust.

Fire is hellfire – evil, sin, damnation, monstrous violence. Fire is torture, the awful martyrdom of Joan of Arc, the conflagration of witches and sodomites, the history of murder and mayhem that has devastated same-sex lovers around the world. Fire is danger – the awful danger we all still face, the pain and torment of contemporary queer martyrs who are bludgeoned to death in Vancouver, stabbed in Montreal, killed by a firebomb in Oregon, imprisoned and stoned in Iran, shot in Serbia, raped and tortured in Brazil.

The AIDS holocaust consumes our community. We grieve until it seems we are ready to erupt in flames. When we are capable of spontaneous combustion, we become fire-breathing dragons, screeching prophesies. We see, as no one else can, clearly into our own times

Il Sodoma (1477 –1549), aka Giovanni Antonio Bazzi, *St. Sebastian* (1525). Galleria degli Uffizi, Florence. The Yorck Project: Wikimedia.

Suffering

"Each solar flare of hatred and fear
I have survived, then sifted the ashes – a prospector.
No fire has destroyed my best and most malleable stuff."

– CRAIG REYNOLDS[1]

Joan of Arc was a peasant girl who heard voices. In 1426, when she was 12 years old, she ran away from home and worked at an inn. Her visions increased, finally urging her to don men's clothes and lead the armies of France. At first the army generals laughed at her, but she began to prophesy, and when her prophesies came true they let her lead the troops. The enemies of France captured her when she was eighteen, and brought her to trial for witchcraft and heresy. Joan of Arc was convicted and condemned to death. At the age of nineteen she was burned alive in the public square. She took hours to die, in terrible agony. Her screams shook the townspeople, as the smell of her burning flesh filled the air.

In 1998 two men beckoned Matthew Shepard, a gay college student, into their truck by pretending to be gay. "Guess what, we're not gay," said one of his attackers, placing his hand on Matthew Shepard's leg. "You're going to get jacked. It's Gay Awareness Week." The men beat Shepard's head with their fists and a revolver. They kicked him repeatedly in the groin. When his head was so bloody they couldn't see his face, they tied the young man to a ranch fence. Matthew Shepard hung there for eighteen hours, in the cold and dark, slowly perishing. Finally he was cut down and taken to a hospital. It took him another four days to die.[2]

We are everywhere, it's true, and there are societies where gender transgression and same-sex love are accepted as part of the spectrum of human capacity, available to all citizens or a chosen few. Not here. Intolerance runs deep in Western culture. The Romans persecuted polysexual pagans and reviled effeminate men, despite the prevalence of same-sex passion. In 6th Century Byzantium Emperor Justinian "ordered that all those found guilty of homosexual relations be castrated. Many were found at the time, and they were castrated and died."[3] In Panama in the 16th century, the Spaniards fed native people accused of sodomitical practices to dogs. Throughout Europe during the Inquisition, Christian witch hunters captured strong women and gentle men. Their fingers were crushed in vices, pieces of their flesh were torn away with red-hot pincers, and they were burned to death. In the 20th century homosexuals were imprisoned, tortured and murdered by Nazis. Those who survived the concentration camps found themselves the only prisoners not entitled to reparation. Many were imprisoned again by post-war German courts.

In the past few years, the news has carried stories of people burned alive for gender transgression, bludgeoned to death for being queer, cut to pieces, buried in sand up to their necks and stoned to death, shot, lynched, firebombed. Homosexuals are fired, driven from their homes and hunted down. Some die by their own hand. Queer youth hang themselves, blow off their heads, and OD on drugs in terrifying numbers. AIDS consumes the most precious, beloved spirits. GLBTQ people carry the burden of this suffering, whether we speak of it or not, whether we give it our attention or avert our gaze. Centuries of suffering smoke and burn inside the marrow of our bones.

What does it mean, to be so menaced? James Baldwin comments, "If one is continually menaced by the worst that life can bring, one eventually ceases to be controlled by a fear of what life can bring. . . ."[4] The fear of suffering paralyzes identity in empty structures of disavowal. Queer people are *annealed* by fire. Instead of being victims of suffering, we can be empowered and enraged by suffering.

Queer people face fear every day. Death is around the corner, inside the mailbox, under the lamppost, in the eyes of the next-door neighbor. Fear keeps our hearing sharp and our eyes clear. It makes our footsteps swift and light. Suffering is our familiar, an intimate spirit at our shoulder who shapes and informs our lives.

"You're pathetic!" teenage bullies say to all the gentle boys and strong girls. Indeed, accepting the joys and risks of queer identity includes accepting pathos as a condition of our lives. The Greek word *pathos* denotes suffering, and also passion, trauma, disorientation, and a visit from the gods. No wonder it is linked with queer identity. A-pathy, its opposite, is irrevocably linked with heterosexual identity in our times.

Heterosexual masculinity is constructed by a repudiation of the pathetic self. Forsaking the arms of the Mother for the name of the Father, men forego feeling, compassion and vulnerability. Apathy is the sign of masculinity. Women are thought to have a privileged access to feeling – inasmuch as they are feminine, they are pathetic. But when they use these pathetic qualities to contrive a relationship with men, to become a commodity that can be evaluated in the patriarchal economy, they alienate their pathos in an object-identity that leaves their strength and independence unexpressed. Femininity is a product of artifice, where suffering, vulnerability and helplessness are externalized and objectified. Apathy is the secret sign of femininity, or as Marilyn Munroe sings it, "Diamonds are a girl's best friend."[5]

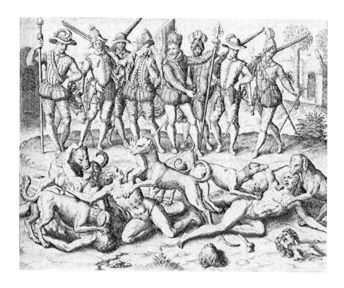

Vasco Núñez de Balboa (ca. 1475 -1519) executing indigenous Panamanians by war dog for same-sex practice. New York Public Library, Rare Book Room, De Bry Collection, New York

Rollo May describes apathy as the withdrawal of feeling, noting that it is linked with violence. He writes, "When inward life dries up, when feeling decreases and apathy increases, when we cannot affect or even genuinely touch another person, violence flares up as a daimonic necessity for contact, a mad desire forcing touch in the most direct way possible."[6] Relations between men who can never touch each other devolve to patterns of apathy and violence. Indeed it is the fear of touch – the phobic repudiation of male-to-male eroticism – that motivates so much violence between men.

When relations between men and women are drawn into the black hole of gender roles, "inward life dries up." They cannot touch each other as human beings with passions and infirmities, capacities and needs. They can only hold the crude effigies of male and female. Apathy and violence are the telling, if not inevitable, marks of heterosexual relationship.[7] It sometimes seems that no matter how hard and soft a man tries and a woman tries to transcend history and culture and do it differently, they get sucked into the vortex. Some humiliation they endure and some privilege they assume feeds the insatiable Hydra of sex and gender.

Homosexuals can let pathos characterize their lives and relationships. We can admit our souls into our conversations. We can admit profound tragedy, as well as transforming passion, into our hearts. Our identity as GLBTQ people is, in part, a relationship with vulnerability and loss. Suffering and death are ever-present as a possible future and a collective past. Even as we fight against the violence which threatens us, we can use suffering as a guide to claiming passionate lives and authentic relationships. Pathos is a pathway to exquisite sensibility. Being queer keeps us fiercely alive.

Chamunda, 11th-12th century, National Museum, Delhi. The ten-armed Chamunda is seated on a corpse, wearing a necklace of severed heads. Photo: Hideyuki Kamon.

Rage

Pele, Hawaii's goddess of volcanic fire, is a hag. Her skin is rough and black. She is a raging, destructive power. Chamunda, an aspect of the Hindu goddess Kali, dances in the cremation ground, eating corpses. Her hunger can never be satisfied. In constant agony, she fills the world with her terrible cries.

These are lesbian images, kindred spirits to all Raging (Lesbian) Feminists, patron saints of s.c.u.m. – the Society for Cutting Up Men.[1] Anger and vengeance are powerful, creative forces in lesbian responses to women's oppression.

Aspects of the gay and lesbian civil rights movement would have us forgo our fury. Dressed in suits and ties, acting like respectable people, we represent ourselves as innocent victims of unjust treatment. Our wounds are honored, but not our rage, hostility, and aggression. In contrast, the Queer movement of the 1990's invoked the archetype of the Destroyer, vivifying LGBTQ identity.

"I HATE STRAIGHTS," the Queer Manifesto of 1990 reads. "They've taught us that good queers don't get mad. They've taught us so well that we not only hide our anger from them, we hide it from each other. WE EVEN HIDE IT FROM OURSELVES. We hide it with substance abuse and suicide and overachieving in the hope of proving our worth. They bash us and stab us and shoot us and bomb us in ever-increasing numbers and still we freak out when angry queers carry banners or signs that say, BASH BACK .... LET YOURSELF BE ANGRY. Let yourself be angry that the price of visibility is the constant threat of violence, anti-queer violence to which practically every segment of this society contributes. Let yourself feel angry that THERE IS NO PLACE IN THE COUNTRY WHERE WE ARE SAFE, no place where we are not targeted for hatred and attack, the self-hatred, the suicide – of the closet."[2]

The Queer Manifesto catches "the pure rage that most of us had learned to swallow," Frank Browning writes.[3] We subdue our anger in the everyday acts of our lives – dropping our lover's hand when we turn the corner, murmuring at pictures of babies we are not allowed to play with, marking all the weddings and anniversaries that celebrate heterosexual privilege, carefully choosing where and when we are open about our evenings, our households, our friends dying in mid-life.

The Queer Manifesto continues, "The next time some straight person comes down on you for being angry, tell them that until things change, you don't need any more evidence that the world turns at your expense .... And tell them not to dismiss you by saying, 'You have rights,' 'You have privileges,' 'You are overreacting,' or 'You have a victim's mentality,' Tell them, 'GO AWAY FROM ME, until YOU can change.'"

The Remorse of Orestes. Orestes is surrounded by the Erinyes, also known as Furies, chthonic deities of vengeance in ancient Greece. Painting by William-Adolphe Bouguereau, 1862. Wikimedia.

Rage is energy that allows us to use queer identity as a profound interrogation of the straight world. If we are mad enough, we can see straight as every unexamined life that reeks of unexamined privilege. Straight is the preposterous designation of sexual difference and in-difference that orders the meaning of everything, from apple pie to urban planning. We want to burn it down, shake it up, tear it to pieces. Like the Ancient Greek Furies, we are FURIOUS. We want justice, ret-ribution, and torment for all who have offended us.

Time after time, GLBTQ people relinquish their rage. We keep greeting homophobia with gentleness, acceptance and love. At what cost? If we always only forgo our anger, we give away our power. Queer rage is what puts deviance back in sight. Anger lets us acknowledge how our passions twist and redirect the meaning of things. Instead of hopelessly affirming that we are ordinary people, we can use homosex-uality to rage against the suffocating weight of ordinariness.

Western culture represses consciousness of all the rage it generates; it has never honored the Destroyer. In Ancient Greece, the Olympian Gods banished the Furies – that fearful lesbian sisterhood with their taste for vengeance.[4] Christianity would also resist or conquer the Destroyer, which is identified with the Devil and with Death. The dream of modern mental health likewise rejects destructive emotions: aggression, hostility, cruelty, anger, revenge, retaliation. These denied emotions return as the unacknowledged shadow, possessing personal and global relationships. Being queer means we can engage the archetype. By entering its mystery, we might assimilate its power, even while we loosen its grip.

Shunga Scroll, Japan, Edo Period. Two women use a Tengu-Mask as a Dildo.

Sex

"The goatlike cry of 'Brother!'
is worse than shouting Fire –
contains more danger. For centuries
now it has been struck out of
our language."

– TENNESSEE WILLIAMS[1]

Public sex, transgressive desires, the orgies of witches, the blood and shit of leathermen – queers tend the sacred fire of sex. We break laws, pass over limits and boundaries, exceed what is possible. However chaste and circumspect our personal lives, just by being queer we invoke for others the heat of Satanic sexual fire. According to the Westboro Baptist Church, homosexuals are "a group of people who BURN in their lust for one another, and who FUEL God's wrath."[2]

A devil buggering a man. India (?), Gouache 19th century. Library reference no.: ICV No 51428 and External Reference 47695i. Wellcome Library, London

Sex turns us upside down and inside out, erasing certainties and separations. Lust burns up the boundaries with which we construct a sense of self, differentiated from the world around us and defended from its incursions. Intercourse opens our bodies to an other and initiates us into a deeper and more terrifying knowledge of self. When sex is hot, we experience disintegrations of body and soul.

Sex is a visceral representation of the opening and surrender that every intimate relationship demands. No profound union with another lets us stay intact and self-identical. We become one pair as well as two individuals. Each one surrenders the carefully constructed ego and its wishes. Joseph Campbell comments, "Marriage is not a simple love affair, it's an ordeal, and the ordeal is the sacrifice of ego to a relationship . . . ."[3] Men and women in sexual relationships with one another may seek to abjure this truth. The social support their sexuality receives can lure them into believing they are safe; there is no risk; nothing will make them bleed and weep. Safety and self-protection become an aim and an end. But without loss and danger, there can be no relationship. Queer means accepting risk as a condition of our lives. We are exposed, injured, and called to union with another greater than ourselves – our lovers, our queer identity. Self-certainty is destroyed in the fire of desire and its social stigma. It matters little that most GLBTQ people want only the most private and polite exchange of kisses and orgasms. Queer identity opens to the archetype of mad illicit passion, impossible pleasure, unwilling surrender, fire, sex.

In the Middle Ages, same-sex lovers called themselves Ganymedes, after the boy who was raped and abducted by Zeus in the form of an eagle. Today the homophobic stereotypes that surround queer identity carry the image of sexual fire for contemporary society: violated children; abusive priests; seduced hockey players; prison rapists; leather dykes; barebacking People with AIDS. No matter how ordinary and obedient our personal sexual choices, we can enjoy the transgressive power that queer identity evokes.

In Central and Northern Europe ecstatic sex was an aspect of pagan ritual worship of the great goddesses of death and fecundity and the green and mortal god. This sex involved the choreographed experience of power and surrender, psychological depatterning, and ecstatic unity with the other. Christians violently repressed these rituals, and the alternate world view they supported and expressed.

Christianity breaks the world into opposites – self and other, good and evil, us and them, heavenly and demonic – without offering techniques of trespass and reasons for reconciliation. Almost all other world views suggest ways to incorporate the shadow, pay homage to the destructive forces that help to shape inner and outer realities, and envision a unity of self and world. Christianity explicitly repudiates this possibility, consigning all that is other and evil to hell. There fire consumes witches, sodomites, savages, and fornicators of all descriptions. Illicit sex represents the danger – and attraction – of lust and appetite that would have us exceed boundaries and enter the opposite. So sex can turn you into a work of fire, in this world, or the next.

Homophobic stereotypes consign us to hell and identify us with evil. We are irredeemably other. Our sex, however ordinary, has at least this transforming power. We are called to use sexual energy as a technique of the spirit, a way to erase boundaries and achieve metamorphosis. Through the fire, we lose our sense of self as a discreet entity. We become water, mud, blood and stone – and we are willing to defend the earth's life with our last breath. Sex is radical, fearsome and dangerous when it evokes this unity with all that is other, opening self to world, and world to self.

A man enjoying an erotic dalliance with two boys, seated on the bank of a pond with lilies, beneath a willow tree. China, Gouache, 19th century. Library reference no.: ICV No 47945, Wellcome Library, London

Pedophilia

Homophobes work tirelessly to prevent gays and lesbians from having access to children. Many of us withdraw voluntarily from the children who could be in our lives. We shrink from the accusation that is always ready-to-hand – pedophilia! Scientific research proves decisively that there is no association between homosexuality and the sexual abuse of children. One study concludes that "a child's risk of being molested by his or her [mother's] heterosexual partner is over 100 times greater than by someone who might be identified as being homosexual, lesbian or bisexual."[1] In fact, children may be safer around gays and lesbians. Gay and lesbian parents are less likely to physically or sexually abuse their children.[2] A survey of child molesters found that none of them were homosexual.[3] But queer has an association with pedophilia that resists the evidence of science. Over half of respondents to opinion surveys believe that gays and lesbians should be prohibited from adopting or even from teaching young children.[4] The media, remaining silent on subject of child neglect, seizes avidly on each detail of the drama when a priest, coach or teacher is accused of same-sex sexual abuse. The spectre of the evil, predatory homosexual looms large in the cultural imagination. We are their worst nightmare. Without their constant vigilance, we might swoop down and abduct every innocent child. Perhaps we can learn to use these vast powers they invest in us.

We might as well admit that pedophilia has a long pedigree within the history of male same-sex passion – much longer than the history of reciprocal, companionate relationships that are typical in contemporary Western queer communities. In other cultures, pederastic relationships are pedagogical. This was true in Ancient Greece. Will Roscoe writes of Japanese samurai warriors who followed *wakshuto*, the way of loving boys, and the Sambian people of New Guinea. In Greek and Roman mythology, the myth of Ganymede exemplifies the archetype. Zeus, king of the gods, was inflamed by a passion for the boy, Ganymede. Zeus transformed into an eagle and abducted the child, carrying him off to Mount Olympus. Once there, Ganymede became immortal, and he serves as cupbearer to the gods. "The myth of Zeus and Ganymede became an important wellspring for images of homosexuality in Western culture," comments Will Roscoe.[5] In the Middle Ages, same-sex lovers called themselves Ganymedes. Historian John Boswell calls the period 1050-1150 "The Triumph of Ganymede," noting the emergence of a "gay subculture" all over Europe wherein Ganymede appears in many guises, usually as a "representative of gay people in general." "In several debates of the period he is a spokesperson for the gay side...."[6]

The notion of a powerful stranger (for eagle, read chicken-hawk) abducting a child who gladly serves him evokes automatic indignation today. "The child" imagined and created by contemporary Western culture is innocent, empty, helpless and sexless. Legally and morally, children are dependent on adult protection. Sex with children is posed as the ultimate taboo. Yet evidence of child molestation is uncovered everywhere. Child sexual abuse seems almost to be a characterizing trait of every cultural institution, from church through family. Child molesters lurk behind every tree, and might be there inside the secret heart of every loving teacher or parent. James Kincaid describes this as a "culture of child molestation," in which children are eroticized and the erotic is infantalized. Every adult-child relationship is scrutinized for a punishable offense. No wonder then, children are unwelcome everywhere. People want movies, dances, apartment blocks, and even whole cities without children.[7]

Late Archaic terracotta statue of Zeus and Ganymede, Olympia Archaeological Museum. Photo: Joan Banjo. Wikimedia

The protection of children has become a protection racket. Children are increasingly guarded, preserved from work and from contact with strangers, and kept close inside the confines of the nuclear family – where they are so much more likely to be abused than anywhere else. The sexual exploitation of children is only possible when they are trapped, abject and dependent. Families ensure children's vulnerability and enforce their compliance. In contemporary industrial society, children have no autonomy. Parents are established as a child's only source of food, shelter, measured affection and brutal punishment. Mothers and fathers are left isolated and without support. Shere Hite comments that the authoritarian, patriarchal structure of the family is designed to teach "that power and might are the most 'real' and important thing in the world."[8] Becoming queer despite our families of origin, we refuse this lesson. We escape the paradigm and prove the alternative. The African proverb "It takes a whole village to raise a single child" is the moral of every queer life story. We are nourished and sustained by nature, books, friends and fabulous strangers as well as – or in spite of – our family of origin. We predict a society released from the tyrannies and oppressions that create child victims when we defy the patriarchal nuclear family with our resilience.

As queers we are called to solidarity with other refused and stigmatized sexualities. In the early years of gay liberation, this meant advocating with young people for age of consent laws to be abolished. It meant support for "Men Loving Boys Loving Men."[9] Lesbian-feminists intervened on behalf of children. They pointed out that sex with children must be exploitative and profoundly damaging in a society where children are silenced and deprived of choice. Gay liberation lost its willingness to speak on child sexuality and pedophilia. We have been content to claim our distance and difference from these issues. In the culture around us, hysterical denunciation of child molesters grows shriller. Castration is advocated and practiced on offenders (as it was on homosexuals in the 1950's). In B.C. in 2002 a man was hounded, vilified, arrested and prosecuted for his creative writing involving fictional characters described as minors.[10] A society that has become hypervigilant towards the rare incidence of the sexual abuse of children by strangers is willfully blind to the relatively common incidence of abuse and neglect by parents. Those who watch waiting to pounce on a hidden pedophile seem content to ignore the all-too-evident children who are hungry, homeless, without clean water, education, or medical care. If GLBTQ liberation is to move us anywhere outside the predictable parameters of acceptability, we need to advocate for the empowerment of children.

Shah Abbas and Wine Boy, Persia, 19th century

Within the archetype of initiation exemplified by the myth of Ganymede, boys become men by having sex with them. In contrast, contemporary Western culture has it that manhood is produced in boys precisely through their repudiation of homosexuality. Being a man means becoming stiff and impenetrable. Little boys are taught to close up their orifices and close down their vulnerable emotions. They are pulled away from their mothers and the world of women. The world of men seduces them – bloodlessly – to an ideal of masculinity, and a realm of power they can access by approximating the ideal. And it scares them. Torture, rape, bashing, murder, social ostracism, psychiatric mistreatment, poverty and marginalization are among the punishments meted out to boys who refuse to assume the masks and postures of masculinity. In the construction of gender, the erotic component of man-boy relationships is forced underground, made into a terrible secret. When pleasure between boys and men is impermissible, the assumption of manhood is made problematic, provisional and disturbed.

Lesbians have been leaders in fighting against the sexual exploitation of children and breaking the silence that surrounds it. Yet we have not flinched from acknowledging the erotic aspects of a mother's relationship with her daughters, of "female friendship and comradeship" (Adrienne Rich),[11] and of "the sharing of joy, whether physical, emotional, psychic, or intellectual" (Audre Lorde).[12] Being and becoming a woman has little to do with relations between women. Girls are "made" into women by submission to heterosexual intercourse.[13] "Woman" names a relationship with men and heterosexuality. And precisely because relations between girls and women take place at the margins of society, without language or consequence, they retain an erotic capacity. "The interplay of desire among women's bodies, sexes and speech is inconceivable in the dominant socio-cultural economy," Luce Irigaray writes.[14] This interplay of desire exists, nevertheless, and not only in the behavior and relationships named homosexual. "The lesbian continuum," as described by Adrienne Rich, implicates all women – "from the infant suckling at her mother's breast, to the grown woman experiencing orgasmic sensations while suckling her own child . . . to two women . . . who share a laboratory, to the woman dying at ninety, touched and handled by women . . . ."[15] Caresses across surfaces – be they of lab or labia – free exchange, pleasure without possession, intergenerational bonding: the lesbian continuum evokes the possibility of a "pedophilia" through which we might re-imagine childhood.

Audre Lorde writes, "Recognizing the power of the erotic within our lives can give us the energy to pursue genuine change within our world, rather than merely settling for a shift of characters in the same weary drama."[16] We can acknowledge a range of erotic feelings in adult-child relationships that is neither criminal nor harmful, but is another aspect of our multiple connections to one another. We can learn to love children enough to safeguard them from actual, verifiable dangers, and still allow them adventure, pleasure, and play. So long as children have no autonomy, perhaps we can preserve them from sex, but without resorting to a hysterical invocation of monsters and victims. We can dare to care for one another outside the nuclear family, which ensures the vulnerability of the children it supervises. Perhaps we might even forgo the bifurcation of humanity that separates needy, endangered children from protective, dangerous adults, and instead envision a continuum of human need that includes the dependence of both young and old, but also the radical independence of youth and mid-life. Perhaps we might start talking, with Shulamith Firestone, "not about sparing children for a few years from the horrors of adult life, but about eliminating those horrors. In a society free from exploitation, children could be like adults (with no exploitation implied) and adults could be like children (with no exploitation implied)."[17] Historically, the erotic quality of intergenerational relationships is a profound source of information, energy and joy for queer people. With this legacy, we may illuminate a way out from the circuit of fear, denial, guilt and punishment that is the contemporary discourse on children and sex.

Hans Baldung (1485–1545). *Hercules and Antaeus*, c. 1530, watercolor on paper, 27.8 × 15.7 cm (10.9 × 6.2 in), Cabinet des estampes et des dessins, Strasbourg.

Danger

Saint Augustine, the Father of Christianity whose contempt for same-sex passion helped shape Christian intolerance, once loved another man. Augustine was devastated when his lover died. Torn apart, in unbearable pain, he turned to the Christian god. After his conversion Augustine came to regret the sexual aspect of his relationship, writing "I contaminated the spring of friendship with the dirt of lust and darkened its brightness with the blackness of desire."[1] Augustine shaped his pain and shame into a weapon. It is still a danger. Betrayal, self-loathing, revenge, the Judas kiss – alongside all the miracles and wonder of queer existence, these destructive patterns persist. How do people who have been so thoroughly associated with evil learn to be good to themselves and each other? With no sense of what is good and right that can embrace us, we can be demoralized. We can stay trapped in self-hatred and internalized homophobia. We can be deprived of spirit, courage and kindness. Or homosexuality can lead us through the fire, to a deeply ethical, yet radically open, way of living in the world.

Ethical behavior is traditionally based on obedience to a code of rules that defines virtue and prohibits vice. For centuries this code has been contrived and derived from gender. A "good woman" and a "good man" are she and he who emphatically disavow a capacity for destabilizing the "natural functions" of their sex. The very word "bad" is derived from the Old English *bæddel* – a derogatory term for sodomites.[2] As queer people, we practice the very possibilities that are prohibited by society's implicit and explicit ethical norms.

It is a dangerous transgression. Shame yawns greedily, ready to devour us. How many queer people internalize a sense of wrongness? Today any queer community newspaper contains advertisements from straight-looking, straight-acting, gay white men seeking same – a mirror image to confirm self-hatred and contempt for queer potentialities. How many of us are lost to self-loathing, fear, humiliation, failure? We succumb to failure of nerve – we cower. We make up a new set of rules delimiting virtue and vice, and use them to punish one another.

As well as an abstract set of rules we cannot follow, ethics is a set of concepts we can scarcely do without. But ethical concepts like "integrity," "honesty" and "altruism" may presume a different sense of self and world than queer people can attain. When boys and girls grow into men and women with different-sex attachments, they are confirmed at every turn by culture and society. The rites and rituals of different-sex dating, mating and marriage confer them place and status in the human community. Boys and girls who aspire to same-sex passions and attachments develop a very different sense of self and world. Dorothy Allison writes, "by the time I understood I was queer, that habit of hiding was deeply set in me, so deeply that it was not a choice but an instinct."[3] We stay hidden, isolated and invisible, or become hyper-vis-

ORIENTATION

ible – as heroes, clowns and victims – roles and offices that are just as lonely and claustrophobic as the closet. The self is incarcerated with secrets and burdened with shame. The yearning to know and be known is frozen and entombed.

How does anyone who grows up queer imagine they have integrity – that they are pure, unbroken, untouched, whole? Honesty means we will not survive; disguise and dissimulation are prerequisites to our existence. And altruism – devotion to the interests of others – is just as impossible, when becoming who we are is what offends. Capacities for moral agency derive from a strong sense of self and engagement with the human community. Queer people grow up deprived of both. We are each torn apart and town away from the social fabric. How then can we develop capacities for ethical behaviors and moral choice?

We can craft and practice an ethics that is informed by the peculiar experience of being queer. The enterprise requires a more complex sense of self and one's engagement with the human community than traditional ethical concepts can presume. For queer people, the self is a locus of possibility, a place of action and change that subverts the social order. This order is heterosexuality; heterosexuality consists of the conventions, rules and economic relationships that form the social environment. Monique Wittig writes of how, one by one, lesbians break the social contract. In our voluntary associations with one another, we imagine a new form of social bond. Wittig writes, ". . . If ultimately we are denied a new social order, which therefore can exist only in words, I will find it in myself."[4] This is not the form of self envisioned by contemporary psychology as a locus of private meanings and unique characteristics withheld from social life. Queer people encounter themselves as something else. Our most intimate passions and personal pleasures invent an outer world that is not yet possible.

We envision social transformation desperately, with our desires, and we envision it playfully, with style. Lesbians in lipstick or lumberjack shirts, gay men in leather or crinolines – the self we present to the world is not self-evident. Style takes the self as a work to be accomplished. Following Michel Foucault, we can see self-fashioning as an

124

opening for creative life.[5] Inventing, costuming, practicing and staging the self, we make a tiny space within the apparatus of power where choice is possible. Being queer is itself an ethical practice; we use our sexuality to craft forms of self and relationship that exceed the evident unfreedoms we inherit.

A complex sense of self, forged in social transformation and self-invention, informs an ethics that is peculiarly queer. For GLBTQ people, goodness does not arrive through silence and self-sacrifice. We gain strength and voice from others' strength and voices. We give space to others when we invent and present ourselves. A queer form of altruism requires neither obedience nor subservience. Living for others is a creative choice, emerging through passions and pleasures. Living for self is not about winning power over others. It means using one's singular voice, across its entire range, to sing the world to life. Care of an unstable, invented self is a key to a rich, multifaceted community, where new kinds of relationships become possible through being queer.

Ethics is visible not only as a code of rules or a series of concepts governing individual behavior. Ethics also consists of the moral climate, the ethical atmosphere of public discourse and institutions. It is this ethical environment we address with the pursuit of political equality for queers. We seek the decriminalization of homosexuality. We want protection from discrimination in housing and employment. We lobby and litigate for an education system that stops terrorizing queer youth. We want the right to marriage and its attendant privileges. Underlying our demands is a passion for justice. And there is a danger. The effort to convert homosexuals into entitled participants in the democratic process can tempt us to renounce our peculiarities. Representing ourselves as a group or category "deserving" equal rights can mean disguising and denying queer difference.

There is a tension between GLBTQ people who seek respect and tolerance for their private passions, and those who see radical meaning in queer difference. On the one hand, respectable queers are the ones who find acceptance and forge alliances. They work patiently to create incremental social change. Eric Clarke cautions that contemporary social tolerance of gays and lesbians effects "the transformation of political aspiration into managed inequity. Tolerance is the ruse by which respect for difference covers over a legitimated disrespect. . . ."[6] To be assimilated, homosexuality must be erased, desexualized and silenced. After a long battle by queers and allies in the church, the Anglican Diocese of New Westminster (Greater Vancouver) passed a resolution in June 2002 permitting (not compelling) parishes to celebrate same-sex unions in quasi-marriage ceremonies. Queer Christians rejoiced. But there are dangers in normalizing our existence. Acceptance comes only at the cost of disavowing morally unworthy – or queer – sexual practices and identities. Commentator Davis Harris writes urging tolerance in a National Post article (June 22nd 2002) titled "Gay Unions Shouldn't Divide the Church.": "The blessing of gay unions should help bring stability to gay relationships. This, in turn, should reduce the spread of various diseases which have a high economic, as well as social cost." Nothing has challenged his negative stereotypes of homosexuality. Yet he promotes acceptance, with the view that through adherence to a heterosexist paradigm we might be de-queered. Deprived of the complex network of allusions and associations that compose his image of (unstable, diseased) homosexuality, we might become almost the same as anyone else. "Good" queers are divided from "bad." Those who can be recuperated to sameness are separated from those who persist in difference. Even the act of granting grudging acceptance to some queers creates and upholds negative stereotypes of homosexuality, while saying that some righteous GLBTQ people do not conform to them. Conformity is a precondition for public presence. Our difference cannot make a difference. Queer rights in this sense require submission to moral regulation that pits us against one another, and against our own capacities for myth and meaning.

Same-sex passions flourish, at all times, in all conditions, no matter what punishments and permissions await us. Our capacity to live despite the absence of an environment of justice affords *telos* – purpose – to queer existence. We are called to create a world where there is safety and security for all of who we are. The ethical environment that homosexuality predicts values equality and not equivalence. Enfranchisement cannot derive from conformity to approved behaviors. Instead, we can invent a sociality where difference makes a difference. Being good can become as multifaceted and fabulous as being gay.

Queer is deeply suspicious of any moral stance. Our suffering and exile are evidence that conventional morality is bunk. The moral climate supports hierarchy and exclusion while paying lip service to democracy and belonging. Virtue is a ruse that makes slaves content to serve. Values alibi inequities. This kind of cynicism at least can free us from the endless treadmill of seeking acceptance. No longer constrained by a need to fit in, we can fly out, and explore the far reaches of queer identity. There is a danger. When we care less, we could be careless. Exiled from the moral majority of fools and bullies, we could pretend to self-sufficiency, admit to needing nothing at all. But if we pretend not to ask and refuse gratitude for the crumbs we are given,[7] we fail to live the paradox of dependence and independence. We cannot be fully independent until we are enmeshed in and supported by a community. We achieve an altruism of living-for-others when we speak for and through our uniqueness. And it is when we give ourselves away in love and community that we come alive to our selves.

Homosexuals are forced to exile, suffering and solitude. We can use these experiences to become careless or de-moralized. Or we can use them to craft a beautiful life, following a path of deep humility. If we are humble, we are willing to receive, to ask, and to learn. We accept change; we are open to a multiplicity of meanings and functions. We are incomplete; we acknowledge need and dependency. We receive and give thanks. This humility queerly leads us to strength and pride. Through humility we become neither powerless victims, nor arrogant self-seekers. Instead we are singular members of a community. In community we share our gifts. We use our desires to weave a world of meaning, where each of us can find the responsibilities and commitments that lead to lasting joy.

Giant female figures, Nanfeng Dragon Kilns in Foshan, China, photo: Penny Robertshaw

Space

Space is the fifth element, where earth, air, fire and water transform into gold, the standard of worth, the measure of value.

To be homosexual is to have no space; inextricable with the notion of homosexuality is its exclusion from both private and public realms. The streets are too dangerous; the wilderness is too demanding; the single-family dwelling is too devoted to reproducing the nuclear family it structures and scrutinizes. Queer liberation is tied to spatial claims, expressed in spatial metaphors: Come out of the closet! We're here; we're queer! We are everywhere!

Sanctuary is space – safe and sacred place, where wild life in all its forms can flourish. Bars, parks, homes, and back alleys can be doorways, opening to another country where we are welcome and unafraid. And there is the space between us, shifting as eyes lock in recognition. Shared sensibility connects us, changing the meaning of the world. Becoming queer, we cross a threshold which queers the world around us. All gender-marked and homosocial spaces are infused with energy and light.

Space is the magic of cities, restored to life by the beloved community. Space is wildness, restored to life by love. We use the transgressive capacities of homosexuality to escape conformity, while still enjoying the pleasures of invisibility and sameness. We make mythic space out of our personal experience. Banished to the margins, we become the circumference.

Lithograph, 1831. Lady Eleanor Butler and Sarah Ponsonby, genteel Irishwomen who eloped to Wales, were famous for their romantic devotion to each other, and became known as the Ladies of Llangollen.

Another Country

"The country that enters us through the language and tongue of a lovher is a country that unites us. The country that enters into us through the beauty of trees, the fragrance of flowers and the shared night is a country that transforms us. The country that enters into us through male politics is a country that divides us. The country that enters into us like dreaming into life is a country that invents itself."

– Nicole Brossard[1]

We dream of another country, where we can be homosexual. The name Lesbian carries this dream. We are citizens of an imaginary country on the Mediterranean Sea, where love between women exists in profusion, in the open air, sun-washed and bright. Lesbians everywhere approximate this utopia with whatever resources we can muster. From the Ladies of Llangollen[2] to the Michigan Womyn's Music Festival, lesbians make lesbian space. New rules of engagement; a different history and culture; a transformation of temperature; the unimaginable opening of possibility: another country "enters into us like dreaming into life."

Giant female figures, Nanfeng Dragon Kilns in Foshan, China, photo: Penny Robertshaw

The country we are born into, or that Brossard says "enters into us through history and its violence,"[3] has no space for these fabulous myths and meanings. Heterosexist assumptions about gender and sexuality structure the physical world. Every existing physical space is simultaneously an ideological space that precludes the existence of queer people. Zoning bylaws enforce the difference between (men's) space for work – the city with its phallic buildings – and (women's) space for living – the suburban home with its cuntlike enclosures. It is impossible to "be" queer in the ideological space of a house. Private homes stink of family life, with all its prohibitions and exclusions. The design of buildings enforces equivalence on all family units, however structured. One cannot "be" queer at work, where sex is not supposed to happen and sexual identity can at best have no meaning or consequence. Nature is produced as an ideological space that proves homosexuality is impossible. City streets are redolent with past and present dangers. The soul of the citizen – worker, voter, universal soldier – may include a predisposition to homosexuality, but there is no space on earth where queer can come to characterize our lives.

In another country, homosexuality is the heart of the matter. The many projects and meanings we are called to – from intergenerational passion to frivolity and innocence – need space to be. Space-making is a primary project for queer people. Without space, we cannot survive.

Utopia is the only place where being queer is completely possible. A picture of the Ladies of Llangollen, in their butch clothes, at home in their library, evokes a world for women that can include love of learning, freedom of movement, and a voluntary relationship of equal partners. Walt Whitman writes:

> "I dreamed of a city where all the men were like brothers,
> O I saw them tenderly love each other –
> I often saw them, in numbers,
> walking hand in hand;
> I dreamed that was the city of robust friends –
> Nothing was greater than manly love –
> it led the rest."[4]

He evokes a world for men that can include tenderness, loyalty, and open affection. These are utopian visions, homeless in the world we know. Each time we represent ourselves and our desires in public language, visual culture, personal space and social relationships, we make an opening, a passageway that leads to another country where there is space for us.

A queer house can be such a passageway. From the outside, it looks the same as any other single-family dwelling. Economically, it functions just like any other. But inside the house where two men or two women share their lives, the house holds densely-layered meanings and utopian visions.

Each queer house is a sanctuary. The walls of the house describe the limits of what enclosed, controlled and private space we can wrest from a dangerous world. Inside, we create a sacred space of permission and safety. Here, wildlife can take refuge. We create home in a profound sense, a place of belonging.

Ceramic vessel with a representation of a sexual scene. Chimú Culture artwork, between 1100 and 1400 A.D, Peru. Museum of the Americas. Photograph: Luis García (Zaqarbal), 17 February 2008. Wikimedia.

Queer space is filled with conversation. Design and atmosphere encourage talk. Queer people cannot silently assume a place in a world that exists without them. Conversation constructs identity, community, self-knowledge, and personal space. Words create worlds.

Each queer home employs the metaphor of the closet. Aaron Betsky writes, "The closet is the architectural equivalent of the Freudian mind. It is the hidden interior where we construct ourselves."[5] Heterosexist space represses this symbolism by inserting coherent passages between inside and outside, an awful continuity between private and public life. Queer space honors interiority with difficult entryways, high thresholds, gradations of intimacy, the judicious disclosure of secrets. The difficulty in representing ourselves as queer in public language and social relationships creates space and distance. Individuality can be refined in space that hides an undisclosed self.

Elemental images, patterns and archetypes resonate through queer space. Our homes can confirm and evoke the power and meaning of the elements. Fireplaces and candles bring sacred fire into our living rooms. Beds are shrines. Rich and abiding contact with water – in pools, ponds, elaborate bathrooms, views, tubs, drinking water – brings unconscious life, and our kinship with all life, on site. Connections with the earth are created by gardens, indoor flowers and plants, decks, entryways and openings that bring the outside in and the inside out. Personal decoration, artifice, and the pleasure we take in making things beautiful, give us air to breathe, just as conversation does. Heterosexist space boxes in and flushes away the world's elemental rhythms. Living queer, we find the wild world confirms and creates us. Making space for intimate and repeated contact with the elements, we are invited to the full dimensions of our lives.

Every queer space opens into the community. The utopian dream of a beloved community is the heart of queer space. House opens to neighbourhood, watershed, ecosystem, globe – and a universe governed by the great queer principles of unity, diversity, equality, celebration, unconditional acceptance, joy. The community is marked on a mental map carried by every queer person. Interconnected maps chart a vast network of places where we are welcome, where we have the power to participate in community affairs, where we can hold hands with our lovers, where we can dance. The territory goes around the world: in any city, in any country, there will be places where we are welcome *because* of our sexual orientation. Being queer, we have the right and the responsibility to enter the community, to dream it and to build it into our homes, our friendships, and our public life.

Queer houses provide home, a space of belonging. They encourage conversation and friendship. Engaging the metaphor of the closet, they support rich and complex individualities. They put us in touch with the elements, connecting us with nature and magic. Opening to the community, they fill us with possibility and love. Queer space challenges and empowers us.

Heterosexist houses impose a superficial order and conformity on the gender drama seething beneath the surface. These houses repress change. They render individual difference meaningless. Men and women relating to one another in the heterosexist space of the single-family dwelling are boxed in, isolated, silenced, held apart from nature and community. Whatever change they can achieve in private space is without consequence in social space and public life, where the institutions and customs that regulate gender subsume their voices and their identities. They lack a door and a pathway to another country.

Queer space creates this opening to another country. Envisioning and approximating a comfortable, gracious, healing and connected world, our homes can suggest Utopia. Another country "enters into us like dreaming into life," challenging the prevailing order in our hearts and imaginations. If another country is unimaginable, we can have no coherent view of the changes we desire. However dissatisfied we are with the state of things, we stay stuck in self-interest, or we seek small improvements and parochial reforms at great cost, with little benefit. Queer homes – tiny city apartments, lesbian communes, spacious country estates, even jail cells – can help us find and hold an alternate world view. Another country is a place where women ride wild horses. Men can be soft and pliant. Nature looks like us. Houses are opened to multiple meanings and functions, intersexual and intergenerational. Cities are magic concentrations of energy and light. Work and love are connected, intricately and intimately, when what we make is not severed from who we are, or can become. The world we envision – with candlelight, a meal for friends, photographs on a wall, a secret cherished – involves gigantic change, the broad social and economic reorganization of society.

Radical envisioning requires space and place. When we hold a sense of the world we want, we can begin to let go of the world we know, despite its demands and urgencies. In small ways, limited and constrained by virtually everything, each queer person can make a home, or an image of home, that empowers broad social change. Entering queer space, we are guided to find, claim, and at last to create a world that is sweet and bold enough for us.

Wild woman with a unicorn (Queen of the Animals from the Small Playing Cards), Engraving, Master F.S (c. 1430-1468), Germany, c. 1461. Paper, 4-1/8 x 2-15/16", New York: Metropolitan Museum of Art, Harris Brisbane Dick Fund

Environments

"Madrone Tree, from your thirsty root
feed my soul as if it were your fruit."

– Robert Duncan[1]

Tangle of branches, thick trunks of ancient trees, smell of earth, birds shrill – this is queer space. Homosexuality is at home in the complexity, diversity, and uncontrolled energy of wildness. In a dark, old forest, sex can also be wild. There are places to hide from scrutiny, where names have no meaning or consequence. Landscaped parks with their manicured lawns are historically created to facilitate police surveillance. Queer desire is aligned with bright green growing things and the intricate fecundity of death.

Within a week of the Stonewall Rebellion, New York 1969, the first gay environmental group was formed. The group, called "Trees for Queens," aimed at restoring a cruising area in Kew Gardens Park, Queens, New York, where extensive tree cutting and violent vigilante attacks had discouraged the presence of gay men.[2] "Trees for Queens" envisioned the restoration of a landscape, as if in anticipation of gay theorist Alexander Wilson's exhortation: "We must build landscapes that heal, connect and empower, that make intelligible our relations with each other and with the natural world: places that welcome and enclose, whose edges and breaks are never without meaning."[3] Even the name of this first gay environmental group suggests with its double-entendre that trees are for Queens – growing on behalf of Queens, in support of them – just as Queens are for trees, and so the wild world is animated, sacred, and full of love for us. "Trees for Queens" still stands as a fine example of what it might mean to queer nature. In the intervening years, many queer people have worked tirelessly to save whales and defend old-growth forests. But queer participation in the environmental movement has rarely challenged the heterosexist imperative through which natural systems are seen and conceived. What would it mean, to take homosexuality as premise and viewpoint?

Homosexuals must bring a particular sensibility to the experience of nature. Abhorred as unnatural, and alternately as bestial, castigated as primitive, and described as the strange fruit of a civilization grown too distant from the earth, we are attuned to the culture of nature. We know that nature is not a timeless essence, separate from human experience. Alexander Wilson writes, "the whole idea of nature as something separate from human experience is a lie. Humans and nature construct one another."[4] The natural world constructed by the modern sensibility is separated, distanced, classified by taxonomizing systems. Nature is observed from the outside, as a world of fact. It offers no omens. It is devoid of human meaning and significance. A love for nature means only a desire to watch it unfolding, or perhaps to preserve it from human intentions. As queers, we are called to experience nature differently – not just through eyes, but also through ears, nose, throat and skin. Walt Whitman writes:

"We become plants, trunks, foliage, roots, bark,
We are bedded in the ground – we are rocks,
We are oaks – we grow in the openings side by side,
. . . . We are also the coarse smut of beasts . . . ."[5]

Wildness is not something we observe, detachedly. It is home; it is a quality of the heart.

How different the wondrous world of queer nature from nature as it is experienced by "the straight mind." Monique Wittig observes that the straight mind forms its idea of nature around an ineluctable heterosexual fact.[6] The obligatory social and sexual relationship between men and women is the inescapable origin and end from which all phenomena are interpreted. Not only is the world ordered by a drive to reproduction and organized in breeding pairs. The whole non-human world is experienced as other. Nature is innocent, violent, illogical, helpless, endangered – in short, female. Man pits himself against it, saves it, deciphers it, fashions it to his needs.

Consider these stories:

God instructed Noah to make an ark for himself, his sons, his wife, and his sons' wives, and two of every sort of thing: fowls, cattle, and every creeping thing of the earth, a male and female of each. A great flood came, and all flesh died that lived upon the earth. Only Noah and everything with him on the ark was saved.

According to a local Coast Salish story of the flood, the people didn't save any animals. Instead they made a huge canoe, big enough to carry every single child. The adults put the children in the canoe with all the food they had, then said goodbye, and drowned. When the water finally receded, the children wound up on Mount Baker, and they started over in the Fraser Valley with nothing but what they had left in the canoe. When the children realized how many animals had perished in the flood, some of them elected to change into animals. The world was replenished by them.[7]

We could say that Noah had to preserve nature because he understood it in heterosexual terms. Noah had no kinship with the animals on his ark. His god had given him dominion over birds, fish and beasts, saying "into your hand are they delivered" (Genesis 9:2). Noah relied on the difference and distance between himself and the animals to secure his power over them, and so he needed to rely on breeding pairs to replenish the drowned earth. The Salish story tells of a very different world, where relationships between creatures are characterized by kinship and transformation.

Two women embracing and using carrots as dildoes. Gouache painting by an Indian painter, between 1800 and 1899, Wellcome Trust, Photo number: L0033073

Through homosexuality we are invited to live in a world ordered by kinship and transformation. The capacity for transformation, that brings us from expected modes of life to something fabulous, also brings us into alignment with the transforming world – its seasonal cycles, flowing rivers, dramas of birth and rebirth. Queer means we challenge borders and erase boundaries that prevent us from becoming one another. Sustaining ourselves and each other, we fit into a complicated web of lifeforms. We transform the established patterns, seek new habitats and abandon some, live and thrive where it seems we cannot. The extraordinary persistence of same-sex passions, through-out history and around the world, is evidence not of reproduction, but of magic.

Modern life deprives people of magic, just as it cleaves them from place. Separated from the earth and one another, they lose the ca-pacity for storytelling, shape-shifting, tracking animals or talking to them. Nature is seen on TV, through a car window, or confined to parks. Wild is a resource and a refuge, never a home. Both the cul-ture which rewards exploitation of nature and the resistance culture of the environmental movement are shaped by this view of nature as other. Being queer allows us to dream and begin an intimate relation-ship with the natural world. Queering nature may mean that instead of preserving or protecting, observing or extracting wildness, we can come home. Mythic, magic, medicinal knowledge of the wild world is part of every human culture with a sense of home. Coming home means recovering these powers in a community that includes every form of life. Home is an idea of nature that admits a place for human capacities and needs, and tells stories of human loyalty and love for plants, animals and water. With homosexuality as our premise and viewpoint, we cannot see human beings as irrevocable enemies of wildness, any more than we can see the wild world as a territory to conquer, or a series of resources to extract. To queer nature is to claim a kinship with all life, embracing the world's diversity and intercon-nectedness. We are wild and wild is us.

Captain Edward G Malindine and Captain J Palmer, No 5 Army, Film & Photographic Unit, early 1945. Photograph HU 102824 from the collections of the Imperial War Museums.

Absence

"This dread of homosexuality makes, of course, no sense if homosexuality really could be limited to those few percent that most population surveys suggest. Homosexuality can only be a global threat if globally present."

– Henning Bech[1]

In Elizabethan England, male friendship was valorized as the highest possible human relation. These friendships were affectionate, erotic, and most certainly involved sex. Sodomy, on the other hand, was demonized, punishable by death. Allan Bray notes that the codes describing friendship and sodomy were virtually identical, but the two were rigorously and anxiously distinguished.[2] Friendship did not cross class difference. Sodomy involved the transgression of social hierarchies. And according to the Elizabethan world view, social hierarchies were simultaneously cosmic hierarchies. Sex and even love between men of different ages and classes had earth-shattering implications. Sodomy admitted a terrifying disorder to the embattled chain of being.

Love relationships, including erotic exchanges, were encouraged in medieval nunneries. But if a woman was found to have penetrated another with an object, she could be put to death.[3] Lillian Faderman writes of love between women from the Renaissance to the present, noting that society appeared to condone romantic friendships and even lesbian sex. But when women wore male dress and usurped masculine privileges, they were persecuted and sometimes executed. Same-sex passions were permissible – but only within limits defined by acquiescence to class and gender hierarchies.

Passionate friendship remained a possibility and even an expectation until homosexuality came on the scene. From the mid-19th century, homosexuality was produced as a concept by social and economic conditions, sexologists, anti-feminists, psychoanalysts, and people who wanted to craft a life around their same-sex attachments. Sex between people of the same gender took on new meanings and consequences with the advent of homosexuality. In prior centuries, the consequences of engaging in acts of sodomy could include exile, imprisonment, torture, castration, and death, but not psychological treatment, scientific scrutiny, and self-acceptance. Delight in flesh within a passionate friendship would not likely demand the break-up of a marriage, the restructuring of identity, and coming out of the closet.

When there is a minority called homosexual, friendships lose their fluidity. Relationships that previously could include interludes of sex in a lifetime of loving become possessed of a need to disavow – or claim – the possibility of same-sex eroticism. In 1852 Emily Dickinson could write unselfconsciously to her beloved sister-in-law, "Susie, will you indeed come home next Saturday, and be my own again, and kiss me as you used to? . . . . I hope for you so much and feel so eager for you, feel that I cannot wait, feel that now I must have you – that the expectation once more to see your face again, makes me feel hot and feverish, and my heart beats so fast . . . ."[4] Dickinson's niece deleted all of the sexual implications from the letters published in the 1920's, aware that love between women was condemned as perversion. The identification and stigmatization of same-sex eroticism as homosexuality, and the corresponding effort to display the absence of sex in same-sex relationships, did not happen all at once and overnight. Even today some passionate friends hang on doggedly to their "innocence," pursuing a range of romantic and sensual expressions without either claiming or repudiating homosexuality.

In a study of the sex life of American white, middle-class women undertaken from 1918 through the 1920's, Katherine Davis found that 50 percent of single women had intense emotional relations with women and 50 percent of these relationships were decidedly sexual. Among married women, 30 percent had fallen in love with other women, and half of these relationships were sexual.[5] Alfred Kinsey, in his research into Sexual Behavior in the Human Male in the 1930's and 1940's, found that 37 percent of men surveyed reported at least one homosexual contact to the point of orgasm. Another ten percent of males were more or less exclusively homosexual for at least three years. He concluded that 50 percent of men had some kind of homosexual experience. Subsequent sex researchers have failed to reproduce these statistics. A 2001 survey of Canadians found that only 2.6% have had a sexual relationship with a person of the same sex (and that no residents of Alberta were among them!). In the USA a 1992 survey found that only 7.1 percent of men and 3.8 percent of women reported some type of sexual contact with a same-sex partner since puberty.[6] It seems that the incidence of same-sex eroticism has significantly declined in the years since Davis and Kinsey did their research. As homosexuality becomes increasingly visible in the culture, it is increasingly absent from same-sex relationships.

When same-sex passions and attachments no longer take place in an unscrutinized, unstigmatized field, the possibility of sex between men and between women declines. Freud remarked in 1915 that "all human beings are capable of making a homosexual object choice and have in fact made one in their unconscious."[7] The possibility and promise of same-sex eroticism is everywhere visible, in sports, movies, advertising, religious imagery, and homosocial environments of work and leisure. Yet these same spaces are governed by what Henning Bech describes as the "imperative of repudiating homosexuality."[8] The possibility of same-sex eroticism is conjured, only to be disavowed. Same-sex sexuality is denied, camouflaged, or blatantly expressed, only to be clearly separated (shown as belonging only to the homosexuals).

Gender-marked and homosocial spaces – locker room, girls' school, sports team, kitchen, army barracks – could, and once did, radiate with erotic energy. These spaces are increasingly marked by what Bech calls "absent homosexuality." Homosexuality is conjured and repudiated, through queer-baiting, posturing about heterosexual conquests, silence about the beauty of each others' bodies. Absent homosexuality affects all friendships. Intimate same-sex relationships must continually repudiate homosexuality, or claim it, or be avoided altogether. Homosexualized, while they are defended against and deprived of homosexuality, intergenerational relationships are seized and destroyed by the awful omnipresence of absent homosexuality. Absent homosexuality becomes an emptiness at the heart of all human relationships.

Bech describes absent homosexuality as "a major organizing power of modern societies, on a par with other great agents such as capital and bureaucracy."[9] Absent homosexuality continually manages the possibility of same-sex eroticism, confining it to ghettoized enclaves and pathologized persons. All same-sex passions are stigmatized. Unlike passionate friends of past centuries, homosexuals constitute a social threat.

The rich history of same-sex passion notwithstanding, previous eras afforded no space for *being* homosexual. Passionate friendships involved sexual acts, not whole identities. When sex between men and between women can happen without being identified as queer, same-sex passions can actually facilitate the functioning of existing class and gender hierarchies. Homosexuality is different from this; it carries within it the radical revisioning of legal, social and institutional limits. Michael Foucault describes it thus: "To be gay is to be in a state of becoming. ... To be gay signifies that [the sexual choices one makes] diffuse themselves across the entire life; it is also a certain manner of refusing the modes of life offered; it is to make a sexual choice into the impetus for a change of existence."[10]

The anxious, desperate, soul-destroying disavowal of homosexuality that confronts us everywhere paradoxically affirms or even creates a radical space for homosexual existence. The fear of homosexuality pervading 21st-century Western culture establishes being queer as a lived otherness with mythic dimensions. Absent homosexuality locates the possibility of homosexuality outside of the homosexuals, effectively queering every human relationship. In the form of disavowal and the presence of absence, we are everywhere. Queer is a state of becoming that we are still calling, as it calls us, into life.

Pilbara rock art region, Australia. Upper Yule River. Two women dancing.

The Body

A queer body is more than an assembly of organs and physiological functions. It is an anomaly, a mystery, a metaphor.

Ordinary human bodies are transparent to their medical certainties. In the mechanistic world-view of modern science, questions about the meaning of life are answered by the body's reproductive functions. Queer bodies refer us to the mystery of origin. What makes us? Why are we here?

Queers cannot automatically assume a gendered body. We have no way to unproblematically "be" men and women. Homosexuality means always flirting with cultural stereotypes, performing gender, and de-naturalizing it. We call the assignment of gender categories into question.

A gay man can assume the clothes and gestures of a woman, but he does not become a woman. Judith Butler observes that drag queens

146

mimic the "structure of impersonation by which any gender is assumed."[1] When a drag-queen sings the feminist anthem "I Am Woman," we laugh at how a woman is contrived. Gay men can also act masculine, but this masculinity appears in a way that again calls gender categories into question. In gay men, masculinity loses its punch. The forms and objects of masculinity stop reading as expressions of power and privilege, and instead become erotic lures. Through gay performances of masculinity, we notice that every man contrives his gender through donning the clothes, postures and privileges of men. All men become visible as male impersonators, acting out the naturalized ideal of what a man is.

Gustave Courbet (1819–1877). *Sleep*, 1866, oil on canvas. 135 cm. x 200 cm.
Petit Palais, Paris

A butch lesbian can likewise assume the clothes and gestures of a man. She can be seen as "masculine"; she looks so powerful, visible and authoritative. A femme lesbian dresses in a skirt, lipstick and high-heeled shoes. She looks almost like an ordinary woman. But lesbian culture understands the butch-femme relationship with gender as creative and complex. Joan Nestle describes femmes and butches as "gender pioneers with a knack for alchemy."[2] While men and women are impaled on opposite poles of sexual difference, butch-femme is "a lesbian-specific way of deconstructing gender that radically reclaims women's erotic energy."[3] Gender is posed as a space of seduction, play and invention.[4] Butch Jan Brown comments, "We become male, but under our own rules. We define the maleness. We invent the men we become."[5]

An ordinary man or woman undertakes gender as a compulsive and compulsory repetition of the "fact" established at birth. The first words spoken of any baby describe their destiny. "He's a boy!" "It's a girl!" One might be a little more or a little less like the stereotypes; no one feels adequately identified by them. The assumption of gender involves impersonating an ideal that no one really inhabits, as Judith Butler says.[6] The butch undertakes gender differently, making her body into a metaphor. She is steel strong and rock hard. She stands for courage, daring, ferocity, the truth of independence, the dream of power. She does not (cannot) become a man in the social and symbolic order. She can only be a sign, a symbol, an aperture opening into the archetype of masculinity. Beside or inside the butch there is always also the femme. The femme does not aspire to be (and cannot be) a woman in the social and symbolic order. She is an outlaw. Because of who she loves, she must be impossibly strong, resilient, radical. Yet she uses femininity as a language with which to represent herself and her desire in erotic relationships. Femme is a symbol of vulnerability, helplessness, the truth of dependence, the dream of surrendered skin. Butch-femme is a way of being that gives weight and resonance to the erotic moment. When we are held in one another's arms, power and surrender can be soul-gifts, not compulsions of class and gender. Courage, compassion, ferocity, tenderness – capacities so profoundly engaged in the erotic moment – are translated into a stance, a relationship, and a subculture. Butch and femme suggest the possibility of life before or after gender – open to the archetypal patterns expressed by male and female, without capitulation to the social designations and compulsions. Being queer, we are called to live with the granite endurance of Stone Butch and the glittering diamond of High Femme, combined in our psyches and relationships.

Vulva, Paléolithique, Musée des antiquités nationales, Saint-Germain-en-Laye,
photo: Calame, Wikimedia

Many other lesbians choose neither butch nor femme. Rather than
building an interrogatory, erotic or playful relationship with gender,
we can seek to refuse it. Saying 'No' to the social, legal and physical
consequences of being a woman, lesbians can become "embodied" in
a profound sense that is unavailable to non-lesbian women. We can
cultivate our body hair, use our muscles, and wear comfortable shoes.
This is a way of refusing to be a woman, refusing the form of a woman's
body that our culture demands. It is also a positive claim to strength,
fur, comfort, and lesbian visibility. Inhabiting our big, tough, hairy
bodies with persistent grace, we embody capacities and autonomies no
ordinary woman can dream of. Women who are not lesbians find their
bodies made into the preserve of medical knowledge. Internal and
external appearances are anatomized, defined, scrutinized, diagnosed
and regulated by biomedical, pharmaceutical and cosmetics industries.
Women's identities devolve to their reproductive organs, and these are
considered the business of every passing stranger, the husband, the

state, the doctor, the pro-life movement, the pro-choice movement. Barbara Duden comments, "woman's body is public space."[7] Lesbians disappear from the equation, slip away from the scrutiny, and then return shrieking complaint – we are invisible! Outside the reproductive imperative, refusing the clothes, gestures, roles and functions that define and confine what a woman is, we are ignored by the vast machinery that produces women. We are not seen, diagnosed, and adjusted by expert knowledge. We are cast upon our own resources. Thanks to double-edged sword of lesbian invisibility, we can assume a private life and feel our bodies as private space in ways no ordinary woman can. Lesbians can suffer without being fixed. We can feel anger and enjoy laughter viscerally and unapologetically. We can have sexual pleasure without concern for pregnancy. Lesbian bodies, as spaces of physicality claimed apart from expert knowledge, can admit embodied emotions.

We may choose to approximate women or to impersonate men, but as lesbians we always dwell in a nether-world of neither-nor. In Herbert Marcuse's phrase, we are "the continuous negation of inadequate existence."[8] Being what a woman is not instead of always only what she is, we confront the totalitarian regime of the given facts with what is excluded by it. If woman's autonomies and capacities ever find space to exist, it will be in bodies built by lesbians.

The Homomonument in Amsterdam, showing the info sign and one of the three triangles. Photo: Paul2. Wikimedia.

Placemaking

With dawn breaking over the Mall in Washington, four eight-person teams began carefully unfolding twenty-four square-foot quilts, each containing thirty-two panels. One person after another stepped up to the microphone, each reading a list of thirty-two names. When the 1987 ceremony was finished, 1,920 memorial panels covered the earth. Between Washington's phallic monuments to power and the war dead, the soft, bright, handmade memorial to gay men dead of AIDS evoked, for a moment, the impossible enormity of loss.

Being queer is characterized by such acts of creating place. We build temporary, provisional and transgressive space in which homosexuality is possible. GLBTQ people have to continually, self-consciously make space in which to exist. Queer space is no sooner built than it disappears: folded up and put away; ghettoized; annihilated by violence;

absorbed by the vast and overwhelming silence of heteronormative thinking. Being queer is thus continually engaged in this act or attitude of building a place for the self and the beloved community. In the design and construction of place, certain patterns persist as ways we tend to shape the world.

Carnival is one such pattern. We create carnival most obviously in marvelous festivities of gay pride, pride marches, the Gay Mardi Gras, the Gay Games. On Halloween, the quintessential gay holiday, we impersonate spirits and devils, satirize gender roles, mock soldiers, police, cowboys, babies, and ourselves. Judy Grahn calls Halloween "the Night of Nights for the Gay Community."[1] Some aspect of carnival is retained in every queer space.

Carnival is exuberant celebration that incorporates both nightmare images and riotous laughter. Subconscious fears, madness, fantasies, hilarity and freakishness all take their space at the carnival. The authors of *A Pattern Language* describe carnival as "the social, outward equivalent of dreaming." They write, "Just as an individual person dreams fantastic happenings to release the inner forces which cannot be encompassed by ordinary events, so too a city needs its dreams."[2] Queers have created carnivalesque space in which cities can dream – in steamy bathhouses, dark catacombs, and bright-lit homes that ring with music and laughter. Instead of dwelling in the suffocating blandness of heterosexist conformity, we build space where people can don masks and discard them. Women on stilts, men with beards and skirts, dykes on bikes, bears, clowns, slaves – all are brought into the mesh. Carnival honors the phantasmagoria of the subconscious. When we incorporate the carnival's magic into the culture we create and the spaces we build, we proceed from our inmost images to our strongest connections out.

Another persistent pattern we use in the construction of gay space can be described as claiming the commons. Seemingly alone among the inhabitants of the modern metropolis, queers inhabit public space. To be queer is to enter the social and political arena, stake a claim on the commons, and redefine the commonweal. Whether lobbying parliamentarians, presenting GLBTQ issues to the local school board, shopping at the community bookstore, or participating in street festivals celebrating gay pride, being queer involves entering and creating public space.

For people who are not queer, public space might be nothing more than a journey from one private space to another. Streets appear soulless and clogged with cars. Homosexuals find it is both dangerous and exhilarating to appear in public. It takes great courage to walk down the street being an effeminate man or a butch woman. Walking arm and arm with a lover, wearing a rainbow flag, or otherwise claiming queer identity in public, we engender debate and perhaps violence. We provoke a scrutiny of social and legal limits. We claim space and create a commons – shared, contested, open space – as a condition of our lives.

The possibility of community resounds in queer neighborhoods. All over North America and Europe, LGBTQ people have settled in abandoned urban spaces and created, with painstaking effort, lively "villages" known for their intense street life. We have colonized rural areas and developed community institutions and services in the far North, East, South and West. People who are not queer may find community is a concept drained of credibility. Value and meaning are stuck in the private sphere, which public life leaves unexpressed. People feel unknown and unrecognized. Their personal choices, passions and heartaches stay mute and unintelligible in the forms of social and political interactions that modern life allows. As queer people, we find our inmost private being – our sexuality, our individuality, our essence – at the core of our call to community.

Building a place for being queer means that we value everyday sacredness. Ordinary acts create space for friendships. Cooking, cleaning, decorating, gardening and homemaking are examples of placemaking work that is commonly devalued. Other people may care only for money and status within institutions, but in this public world, GLBTQ people are always endangered. Our homes are sanctuaries that nourish and sustain us. Creating retreats from danger, and habitats where gaiety can flourish, means valuing everyday sacredness. Simple acts of grace and kindness, a gentle voice, a carefully-made garment, a vase of flowers, a comfortable meal – all build space and place where being queer is possible.

As queer people build space in which to live, we consistently incorporate a place for the dead. "No people who turn their backs on death can be alive,"[3] write the authors of *A Pattern Language*. "The presence of the dead among the living will be a daily fact in any society which encourages its people to live." Angels fly through the opening ceremonies of the Gay Games. ACT-UP confronts the Food and Drug Administration with a die-in. The *Names Project Quilt* is a radical reclamation of art for human and social purposes. It comforts our spirits; it admits the enormity of our inconsolable grief. When Barbara Deming died of cancer, she left not only her writing but also a fund called "Money for Women," which assists women in their creative projects. *Cancer in Two Voices*[4] is the compelling document of a lesbian couple coming to terms with death. Though we are a people virtually without a history, deprived of human ancestors, we already have graveyards full of guardian spirits. In a society that would turn its back on death, we remember. We mourn. We accept the presence of the dead inside our call to life, to love, and to community.

Pride is a basic pattern queer people use to create space in which to detoxify from heterosexist culture. We celebrate gay pride at rallies, dances, festivals, and by making "wild, mad, revolutionary love" (Jim Fouratt).[5] Bumper stickers, buttons and T-Shirts proclaim our pride. Pride means self-respect and more. It means we can delight in what is peculiarly queer about us. We learn to esteem the rich and complex calling that homosexuality can signify. We find joy in each other, and we find ourselves in this joy – the beauty, strength, giddy laughter, and searing prophesy I honour in you is also a sign of my self. We find a sense of continuity and soulfulness in the history and mythology of same-sex passion. Through pride we choose autonomy instead of shame and doubt. We prefer intimacy to isolation. We live with integrity, instead of despair. Pride can also be defined as arrogance and self-seeking. Pride can be an antonym to the humility we need to live carefully in community. But queer pride is not pride in oneself. Our pride cannot exist without finding and claiming our community. This, if nothing else, might keep us humble.

We build with pride between and alongside invisibility. Being queer involves continual acts of disclosure punctuated by spaces in which we disappear. Yet acceptance, identification and sameness offer their own pleasures and politics. Elsie Jay cautions that we lose "a whole array of invisible activities and the politics of commonality"[6] by an exclusive focus on visibility. Queer pride is built in public space. Rally, ghetto and commercial strip are valorized by a focus on difference. Equally important are the micropolitics of sameness, through which we build home and neighbourhood outside identifiably queer space. When other alliances and identifications claim us, queer identity is slippery and cunning. Behind motherhood, class, color, shared neighbourhood, or shared environmental concerns, being queer can metamorphose into a friendly ghost. Instead of disappearing utterly, or blocking the truth of our commonality, homosexuality forms a transparency that we see through, and are seen through, and that sees us through identification, invisibility and sameness.

Even in enemy territory, we can create queer zones in the space between us. At the railway station, grocery store, PTA meeting, or doctor's office, space is encircled, embraced, and marked off as a distinct region when we recognize one another. Finding strangers with whom to have sex is a dramatic use of this cognitive process. Aaron Betsky writes, "At its most basic, cruising is an activity not unlike that of an aboriginal walkabout, in which the world becomes a score or script that one must bring alive by walking in it."[7] Cruising is only a succinct expression of a function and office every homosexual engages. Whether or not we open our lives to the possibility of sex with strangers, we still bring the world alive by walking in it. In a world of ordinary people, objects and spaces, a queer person can find openings and alleyways that lead to both thrill and danger. Recognition and invitation bring the world to life. Instead of experiencing superficial interactions with a world of dead issues and fixed meanings, we find astonishment. In the space between us, gender has no more regulatory function. Wildness can flourish. There is a place for deep roots, silence and clarity. The space between us is where we find queer identity, and the whole web of mythological associations, cultural expectations, and social possibilities that come with it. Across the earth, in the space between us, the world is wakened from its slumber. Provisional, ephemeral queer zones crackle with electricity. Here, everything is possible. Mobility, fluidity and surprise characterize queer space. We are a people who cannot exist apart from one another. In the recognition by which we call each other into being, we conjure the hope and heart of a living world.

We are building, brick by brick, a world to contain us. The space we make is alive with carnival. We create community from our inmost hearts. We construct a commons in every public space. We value everyday sacredness and incorporate a place for the dead. We shape the places we inhabit with both pride and invisibility. We enter queer potentialities in the space between us.

The authors of *A Pattern Language* describe a view of building that has great resonance for lesbian and gay people. They write, "when you build a thing you cannot merely build that thing in isolation, but must also repair the world around it, and within it, so that the larger world at that one place becomes more coherent, and more whole."[8] Individually and together, we build space to be all of who we are. Everywhere, the world resists us. Yet each small act of building a place for self and community helps to create larger, global patterns. Slowly and surely, piece by piece, we make a world that has these patterns in it.

Bronze man and centaur, mid-8th century B.C. Greek, Bronze, H. 4 3/8 in. (11.10 cm).
Metropolitan Museum of Art. Gift of J. Pierpont Morgan, 1917.
Accession Number: 17.190.2072

Limits

"But I will not agree to be tolerated. This
damages my love of love and of liberty."

– JEAN COCTEAU[1]

Homosexuals are outcasts and scapegoats for contemporary society.
We carry the sins of the people into the wilderness, outside the limits, to the margins where we are made to dwell. This exclusion is not
just involuntary; it is always also constituted by our escape and refusal. Queer is a form of resistance. Moreover, it is a form whose content is inexorably shaped by this resistance. Every image, pattern and
archetype that reflects or evokes queer identity takes meaning from
transgression. Queer is outside, distant to and different from the normal, expected modes of life. Exceeding limits, opening boundaries and
dissolving stable identities are all functions of homosexuality. As an

attitude, orientation, ethos and ontology, queer escapes closure.

Queers represent the liminal realm. We stand on the threshold, leaving one space and not yet, perhaps not ever, entering another. The Greek god of limits and thresholds is Hermes. He presides over crossroads, communication and homoerotic love. He mediates between men and gods and guides souls from this life to the next. Lodging in the space between established alternatives – male and female, visible and invisible, possible and impossible – queer people stand at the crossroads. We guide souls from the constricting limits of what is, to the unknown, unknowable, but nevertheless yearned-for possibility of going beyond this.

If so much of the meaning of being queer derives from our transgression of established norms and boundaries, what happens in those few places where homosexuality is at least partially accepted as a mere difference in taste? In Canada, a decline in the prestige of the family has created conditions for the legal recognition of same-sex relationships as a kind of family. Can we envision a utopia where homosexuality is an ordinary and accepted lifestyle choice? Do we look to the disappearance of queer meanings in places and times where same-sex lovers can live quietly, without fear, or at least without any more fear than anyone else? In the almost unimaginable event that homosexuality is seen as only a matter of taste, like preferring pineapple to potatoes, then opportunities for being queer are divided even as opportunities for homosexual experience are multiplied. Queer is so much more than sex or relationship. Lesbian is an archetype that is stronger and weaker, older and younger than any lesbian. Gay is a dream and a promise that exceeds the limits of any individual, culture or community. If we always only aspire to tolerance and integration, then the mythic journey we bid the world to undertake will stop before it begins.

Where homosexuality is located as a different flavor or a niche market, it seems there is only another way of constructing a society deprived of homosexuality. We can be accepted, but only if the meaning and magic of being queer is evacuated. Such a society is safer, and certainly worth fighting for, especially if we can use these moments of relative freedom to construct and elaborate the queer space we yearn for. There our passion is not for tolerance or integration. We want nothing less than the complete homosexualization of society. We would open every life to the calling that being queer can signify. We would liberate all life to the fabulous queer world we could be playing in.[2]

In a queer world, there is no more evil. Evil has many forms, but they are all inimical to self-sacrifice.[3] Fostering dependency, seeking control of others, and discouraging independence can be evil. Evil can mean succumbing to tyranny, failing to think and act for the self. And it can involve eschewing dependency, being self-ish, failing to live in relationship. Evil is constituted in a failure of love. Only love understands how the self finds its best expression in self-sacrifice – that is, only love as it is practiced by queer people. Without evil, there can be no more whiteness. Like heterosexuality, whiteness is a system of dominance and disavowal that cannot exist in a world of love. Without evil, there can be no more gender as we know it. In a queer world, we could play with gender as a symbolic language and a creative resource, or we could abandon it utterly. And without evil, there can be no more childhood as we know it. In a queer world, both children and adults could be cared for and courageous, frolicsome and beloved.

A queer world is wild. Its most telling quality is aliveness. Being queer means being attuned and responsible to the intricate web of life. We live in community with plants and insects, animals and fish. We are alive in and dependent on water, earth, air, fire. Sensuous, intimate, elemental knowledge of the natural world shapes our being as queer people.

A queer world is created and creative. Becoming queer means surrendering to a higher power, following an inner spirit, undertaking a shaman's journey to identity. On the way we learn to be shape-shifters. We develop capacities for self-invention and for silence. We use art, artifice and artificiality to make a home in the world.

Being queer will find its limit when the world is queer. This cannot only be when everyone savors the delicious taste of homosexuality. Homosexuality calls us to a world that would be unimaginable, if not for the magic, mythic journey of being queer.

Yoruba shrine carving with erotic fertility theme. Photographer: Werner Forman

Stereotypes, Archetypes and Activism

"We are your worst nightmare."

– QUEER NATION SLOGAN

In a 2001 survey of "Canadian Perceptions of Homosexuality,"[1] people across the country were asked, "In your opinion, are homosexuals the same as everyone else?" 77% of those surveyed answered "Yes." The notion that homosexuals are the same as everyone else (save for the unimportant little fact of who we love) is often advanced by queers in search of tolerance. Remarkably, it seems nearly to be established as a definitive statement about who we are. This hard-won form of provisional acceptance has led to the reversal of many legal inequalities. In the summer of 2003, Canadian courts made rulings that allow people of the same gender to marry one another. The U.S. Supreme Court struck down anti-sodomy laws that still criminalize homosexuality in 13 states. Yet the strategically important notion of homosexual sameness has profoundly failed to counter all the forces marshaled against us. In Canada a research paper estimates that homophobia results in 5500 unnecessary deaths each year.[2] Anti-gay hate crimes have risen in recent years, becoming both more frequent and more violent.[3] Homophobic stereotypes continue to proliferate – they are everywhere and overwhelming. The CBC news reports that intolerance is rising.[4] In schools across North America, "That's so gay!" is the most common insult and "Faggot!" the most brutal invective. By Grade 8, 97% of all students have experienced homophobic name-calling.[5] There is a vast and dangerous divide between the notion that queer people are the same as everyone else, and acceptance of the social and cultural difference that is homosexuality.

Homosexuality is not just the unimportant little fact of who we love. It is also the extravagant range and depth of meanings that homophobia attaches to us. Homophobia lives in each cultural image and social interaction. It shapes gender. It becomes a constituent part of family, nature, friendship, race and place. Queer meanings are also made by GLBTQ people – in our acts, attitudes, communities, cultures and histories of difference. We can see that queer is this constellation of meanings continually being made and re-made, instead of (only) an ignorable peculiarity encoded in our DNA. Homophobic stereotypes are a hated source of oppression. Nevertheless, these stereotypes preserve queer difference, proving *ad nauseum* that homosexuality does not fit comfortably with the dominant culture. Queer resistance transforms wounding stereotypes into empowering archetypes that help us think differently, more radically, about our social function.

Homophobic stereotypes refer to interconnected areas of cultural anxiety. Gender is one space of great unease for contemporary society, in which we are confronted with the homophobic stereotypes of the big, butch, man-hating lesbian and the swishy, effeminate gay man. If we keep our response to homophobic stereotypes at the level of stereotypical responses, we valorize gender conformity and "straight-looking, straight-acting" gays and lesbians. There are plenty of us, and in recent years gender-conforming queers seem to have become preferred spokespeople for our communities. But if we reach through the homophobic stereotypes to embrace the submerged archetypes, we will find goddesses who point to women's capacity for anger and vengeance, like Medusa (Ancient Greece), Sedna (Inuit), and Chamunda (India). We find effeminate gods like Bes, from Ancient Egypt, whose breasts gave the first drink, or Jesus, whose wounds evoke a penetration and violation of the masculine image. Through these archetypes, we can see why the homophobes fear us. Homosexuality calls us to a world where women are powerful and men are wounded. Queer points the way to a radical revisioning of the sex-gender system. By attention to refused archetypes that shape the cultural construction of homosexuality, we can embrace gender fluidity and fight for gender equity.

Bradshaw rock paintings in the Kimberley region of Western Australia, taken at a site off Kalumburu Road near the King Edward River.

The relationship with nature is another, related area of deep unease for contemporary industrial society. Here again we are confronted with homophobic stereotypes. We are called "freaks of nature" and a "biological error." We can meet these homophobic stereotypes with plenty of evidence of homosexuality in nature, and claim a counter-stereotype – we are "born that way." But surely it is more powerful, and more interesting, to address the reasons why the charge we are "unnatural" persists despite the evidence. Homophobes want nature bifurcated into male and female, so that the culture of nature props up the sex-gender system. Queer demands something otherwise, symbolized by the ancient archetype of gender transgression. A mask of a woman in childbirth worn by male dancers of the Yoruba tribe, or the woman who wields a triple phallus in an amulet from ancient England, point us to a way of revisioning nature. What would nature look like, if gender transgression was sought and interwoven with desire and culture, ritual and sex? If queer is nature, then nature is polysexual and exuberant. The nuclear family is not after all the inevitable model for love and breeding. The homophobes describe a natural world ordered by competition and reproductive usefulness. It is a view that would have nature mirror the social regime of contemporary society, while it justifies the pillage of an insensate earth. Queer evokes archetypes of cross-species sexuality and animal ancestors, and so a world of nature that is emotionally complex and culturally intricate. Through embracing the refused archetypes behind the homophobic stereotypes, we can create queer as a lived understanding of biological diversity. Homosexuality is a call to act and advocate for the wild.

Another area of profound social unease is the family. A host of homophobic stereotypes fall under this rubric – that we are unstable and immature, that we have dysfunctional, impermanent relationships, that we undermine the family. In the homophobes' heated "Defense of Marriage" from claims by same-sex couples for equal rights, we can see the instability of the family as a social construct.[6] The loving same-sex couple is itself an ancient archetype. Images from around the world and throughout time show a same-sex couple joined at the hips. In pursuing legal equality for queer relationships, we need not forget that the archetype has always signified something different from marriage and family life. Same-sex couples like David and Jonathan, Gilgamesh and Enkidu, Demeter and Persephone or Ruth and Naomi signify friendship, joy, twinship, passion, pleasure without possession. Securing legal recognition for same-sex relationships is important work. But we abdicate the powerful cultural meanings that inhere in our relationships when we counter homophobic stereotypes by claiming adherence to heteronormative values. The nuclear family is an unstable and dangerous construct that keeps its adherents lonely and vulnerable. It is the space where elders, wives and children are isolated and abused. Single folk are pitied and prevented from accessing the family's economic benefits. When we are empowered by the ancient archetype of the loving same-sex couple, we can honor the alternate forms of love and belonging we create in queer community. Communal kinship patterns and partner equity are queer family traditions. We can fight against the oppressions signified by the patriarchal nuclear family, becoming advocates for the rights of children, elders, women and single people. We can honour the new kind of multi-generational, multi-sexual queer families we have made. The construction of homosexuality as a constellation of meanings that undermine the family invites us to shift the focus of queer activism. In addition to the legal fight for equal marriage rights, we can fight against the hegemony of heterosexist family values.

Kitagawa Utamaro (1753 – 1806). *Male Couple*, c. 1802. Half-size oban horizontal yoko-e, 16.3 x 36.2 cms, woodblock color print

Never too far behind the stereotypes that shrill against us is the persistent, terrifying spectre of the homosexual pedophile. One can hardly open a newspaper without encountering this bogeyman. We can be content to counter the homophobic stereotype of the homosexual pedophile with the blameless facts. Science proves there is no link between homosexuality and pedophilia, and suggests that children are actually much safer around gays and lesbians.[7] And we can move to use this homophobic stereotype as a source of power and a path to insight. The pedophile refers to the ancient archetype of initiation. Zeus and Ganymede is one story of a child's initiation to larger dimensions than the family allows. In traditional Zande culture of central Africa, warriors married boys who served them as lovers and helpers, until they became warriors, and married boys themselves.[8] This pattern of same-sex sexuality as an aspect of initiation is repeated in cultures around the world. Will Roscoe notes that the archetype of initiation links gay experience with the shaman's journey, which also involves submission, a shattering of the ego, and a return.[9] Homosexuality signifies a life that is open to risk and upheaval.

The archetype of initiation might encourage us to create a new discourse on child sexuality and youth empowerment. We could be emboldened to fight age-of-consent laws that discriminate against queer youth, and laws against child pornography that are blunt and brutal weapons against queer cultural expressions. We could begin to affirm children's sexuality and protect their gender fluidity. We could move to fight child sexual abuse where it actually, scientifically can be shown to occur inside the patriarchal nuclear family – by fighting the society that keeps children so voiceless and oppressed. On a personal level, this could mean we become scout leaders, teachers, aunties, mentors and guardians who offer children life outside their family of origin. On a community level, this could mean building extra-familial support systems for children and youth, creating oppositional spaces and alternative cultures where children have freedoms and rights.

Morality is another area of social unease that constellates homophobic stereotypes. In popular culture and the homophobic imagination, queer is inevitably linked with sex and violence. We can meet the ubiquitous stereotypes – prison rapists, lesbian serial killers, sex-crazed People With AIDS – with conformist counter-stereotypes.

Bland, innocent, professional, straight-looking, girl-next-door homosexuals prove effective spokespeople for queer rights. And yet this effort – often undertaken at great cost to the representative specimen

– seems only to feed the function of homophobia. Jerry Falwell says we are "brute beasts…part of a vile and satanic system…." Pat Robertson links us with the Antichrist.[10] We can see homosexuals as the innocent victims of unjust stereotyping, and simultaneously follow the stereotypes as maps that lead to buried treasure – the cultural meanings and social power of homosexuality.

Woman spying on male lovers, Qing-Dynasty,
Chinese Sexual Culture Museum, Shanghai

Gigantic sexual energy is an ancient doorway to the sacred. Queer sex, celebrated in other ancient and prehistoric images from around the world, is an aspect of ritual worship in many cultures. Sex can connect humans with the energy of green and growing things, and to the Earth's deep mysteries.

Among the archetypes associated with sexual morality we see how homophobic stereotypes are interwoven with racial stereotypes. Ancient and modern images show racialized others as sexual perverts, pointing to how closely queer liberation is linked with the liberation of other stigmatized identities. The exotic, erotic life of racialized others is queer; queer is darkness, slime, sin and shadow. Creatures of carnival, darkness and depravity have an ancient and enduring association with same-sex sexuality. If we reach down into the archetypal realm for our response to these demeaning stereotypes, we can be empowered by shadow archetypes. The shadow requires attention. We can attend through denial, so that evil is expressed only in pathologies and exorcised with self-righteousness. The shadow can occupy us as a cultural and political regime bent on claiming power over stigmatized others. Or we can admit the refused shadow and integrate the Beast that homophobia and racism both project onto an other.

When claiming power is claiming sameness, we have a simple reverse discourse that operates at the level of stereotype / counter-stereotype. For homosexual activists, this can mean refusing and denying darkness, just as for anti-racist activists it can mean refusing or denying homosexuality. The public face of queer is whitewashed, while racialized minorities are fetishized and sexualized inside queer communities. Homophobia in racialized communities becomes part of an anti-imperialist effort to resist racial stereotyping. Queer people of colour are multiply excluded, jeopardized and disavowed, while white queers get stuck in commodified identities – obedient consumers and producers of the repressive regime of white racial supremacy. The archetypes behind the stereotypes can point the way to a new activism, in which difference is interwoven and sought.

Empowering ourselves and our communities in ways that are informed by difference, we also honour elders and understand the past. From its first beginnings, the discourse of homosexual liberation has been woven of two parts. On the one hand, GLBTQ people have worked towards the naturalization of homosexuality, seeking integration with the whole of humanity. On the other hand, we pose and celebrate ourselves as leaders and visionaries, whose acts, habits and histories point the way to a new social order. In 1894 Edward Carpenter writes, "[It] is possible that the Uranian [(homosexual)] spirit may lead to something like a general enthusiasm of Humanity, and that the Uranian people may be destined to form the advance guard of that great movement which will one day transform the common life by substituting the bond of personal affection and compassion for the monetary, legal and other external ties which now control and confine society."[11] The Mattachine Society, the first ongoing gay rights organization in the USA, founded by Harry Hay in 1948, was based on "a great transcendent dream of what being gay was all about."[12] As the society grew, it began to concern itself primarily with legal change. Hay and fellow visionaries withdrew in disillusion. Hay comments that the group became concerned "with being seen as respectable – rather than self-respecting."[13] The Gay Liberation Front, founded in New York following the Stonewall uprising of 1969, tied gay liberation to peace, racial equality, and a generalized critique of capitalist society. The AIDS Coalition to Unleash Power (ACT-UP) and Queer Nation pursued queer rights through a sophisticated resistance to homophobic meanings. Die-ins of the 1980's and kiss-ins of the 1990's addressed the homophobic structure of physical space. Queer Nation slogans like "We are your worst nightmare" evoke the cultural power of homosexuality.

The radical current in queer activism seems to persist in brilliant but short-lived bursts that are quickly subsumed by a stronger current propelling us to seek accommodation within the dominant culture. The tension between these two currents can be productive and challenging. Joseph Campbell speaks of "two ways to live a mythologically grounded life." He identifies "the way of the village compound," and comments that "remaining within the sphere of your people …. can be a very strong and powerful and noble life." But for those who are called outside the village, and who have the guts to follow the risk, "life opens, opens, opens up all along the line."[14] Queers are ordinary people – mothers, waiters, judges and carpenters. Within the sphere of the village compound, we want nothing more or less than acceptance for all of who we are. And queer is a constellation of meanings that calls us outside the sphere of ordinary life. We are a way of opening to a host of unrecognized, pressing energies that are creative forces for social change.

Legally mandated civil rights for homosexuals will not dispense with queer oppressions. Legislated equality has not produced actual equality for black people in North America, though it has changed the way racism functions. bell hooks writes, "Once laws desegregated the country, new strategies had to be developed to keep black folks in place." hooks sees these strategies as largely cultural, noting "It was easier for black folks to create positive images of ourselves when we were not daily bombarded with negative screen images."[15] So long as homosexuality was segregated and silent, we had some space – however precarious – of solace and self-actualization. Today we encounter innumerable mass-media representations of queer folk, endlessly reproducing the dilemma of stereotype / counter-stereotype. On the one hand, homosexuals are loveless, silly, evil, secret, savage, self-hating and socially isolated. On the other hand, they are bland, white, straight-looking, born-that-way, middle-class and sexually deprived. We are urged to internalize these options, shame queers who do not conform to the counter-stereotypes, and hold a secret sense of wrongness for whatever part of ourselves resists coercion.

Gary Kinsman notes that homosexuality is organized in relationship to all other forms of oppression and dominance, so that class, race and police oppression are manifestly queer issues. The current focus of activism on becoming citizens with equal rights creates two classes of queer people. Economically advantaged GLBTQ people benefit from legal change. Impoverished, young, queers of colour, activist, homeless and gender-transgressing queers are repudiated and ignored in the effort to sanitize and domesticate queer identity.[16] An activism informed by difference urges a different strategy, linking social, economic and environmental rights with individual civil rights. It requires our commitment to understanding and fighting systemic oppressions. In this view, queer difference is not a barrier to overcome. It is a joyful practice of resistance.

Claiming queer identity does not automatically make us politically radical. It scarcely sets us against the dominant culture, if we seek only integration, naturalization, and capitulation to its norms and values. But queer is a constellation of cultural meanings that invites us to opposition. We can be a site of radical disharmony with gender roles, conventional morality, the patriarchal nuclear family, the prevailing culture of nature, and white racial supremacy. Queer in this sense is not something we are born to. It is an imaginative engagement with the cultural production of homosexuality.

Bronze amulet, Woman wielding a Triple Phallus, Bury St. Edmunds, Suffolk

If we attend to homophobic stereotypes, we see queer is not and cannot be made unimportant. As activists, we can only choose whether or not to embrace and use its importance. We can seek acceptance through representations that effect a disavowal of homosexual meanings. We can look to deconstruct and demystify queer capacities. Or we can embrace the socially constructed identity of homosexuality as an opportunity for further construction, meaning-making, and elaboration. We can use queer as a space of agency and a form of power. With our backs against the wall of heterosexist conformity, we can hear the music and dance.

Notes

Introduction

1   In 2015 I was invited to serve as a resource person by students organizing a "sex education" day at the local high school. The students eloquently described the pain of coming of age under the suffocating weight of stereotypes policing gender and sexual orientation.

2   See Didi Herman, "The Gay Agenda is the Devil's Agenda."

3   Bech, 1997, (186).

4   Sadie Fields, quoted in MacLeans', March 29, 2004, p. 26.

5   Jung, Carl G. and Carl Kerényi, 1949, (72).

6   ibid., (79).

7   In Gayatri Spivak's phrase. Stuart Hall, 1989, writes, "where would we be, as bell hooks once remarked, without a touch of essentialism… or what Gayatri Spivak calls 'strategic essentialism', a necessary moment?" (472).

8   Stuart Hall, ed., 1996, (4).

9   Audre Lorde, 1984, (111).

10   David Halperin (1995) describes Michel Foucault's informing notion of homosexuality: "Homosexuality for Foucault is a spiritual exercise insofar as it consists in an art or style of life through which individuals transform their modes of existence and, ultimately, themselves. Homosexuality is not a psychological condition that we discover but a way of being that we practice in order to redefine the meaning of who we are and what we do, and in order to make ourselves and the world more gay; as such, it constitutes a modern form of ascesis. Foucault proposes that instead of treating homosexuality as an occasion to articulate the secret truth of our own desires, we might ask ourselves, "what sorts of relations can be invented, multiplied, modulated through [our] homosexuality…."

Water

1   Hilary Stewart, 1977, (168).

2   This idea originates with Rollo May, 1991.

The River

1   Hilary Stewart, 1977, (168).

2   This idea originates with Rollo May, 1991.

Fluidity

1   As, for example, among the Sambian people of New Guinea where sex between men and boys is universally practiced and endowed with vital religious and cultural meanings, as studied by anthropologist Gilbert Herdt. See Mondimore, 1996, (15-18).

2   An article titled "Study Links Ears, sexual preference" in the Province newspaper (March 3, 1998, A15) describes a difference in the sensitivity of the inner ears of lesbians and heterosexual women. "Now researchers at the University of Texas, Austin, said they found the inner ears of female homosexuals have undergone 'masculinization,' probably from hormone exposure before birth." Simon LeVay (1996) is the author of the hypothalamus study. David Halperin (1995) describes the appearance in San Francisco of a new gay disco called Club Hypothalamus, shortly after the publication of LeVay's notorious study. He writes, "The point was clearly to reclaim a word that had contributed to our scientific objectification, to the remedicalization of sexual orientation, and to transform it ludicrously into a badge of gay identity and a vehicle of queer pleasure." (48).

3   Adrienne Rich, 1986, (34); (50).

4   Sigmund Freud, letter to Wilhelm Fliess, October 17, 1899, quoted by Christine Downing, 1989, (50).

5   Harry Hay, in Mark Thompson, 1987, (198).

6   Walt Whitman, "To A Stranger," Calamus Cluster, Leaves of Grass, Fredson Bowers, ed., 1955, (105).

7   Martha Shelley, 1972 Gay Liberation Classic Out of the Closets Jay and Young eds, reprinted 1992, quoted in Annamarie Jagose, 1996, (40).

8   Will Roscoe, 1998, (45).

9   Gary Snyder, 1992, (271).

The Sea

1   Monique Wittig, 1993, (13); (20).

2   ibid., (32).

3   Thank you to Paula Stromberg for pointing this out.

Surfaces

1   Robert Byrne, ed.

2   This idea is derived from Thomas Moore, 1992.

3   Jacques Lacan, 1977, (1-7).

4   ibid. (7).

5   Paul Monette, 1992, (144).

The Aquifer

1 James Baldwin, 1985, (375).
2 quoted in "Today's Outlook" 1998 Calendar, Nov. 6-7.
3 Robert Hopke in conversation with Mark Thompson, 1994 explores The Wizard of Oz as a gay myth.
4 Carol Warren, 1974, (145) or (162).
5 This is a question asked by Michel Foucault.
6 Mark Thompson, ed., 1984, (265).
7 Aaron Betsky, 1997, (265).

Slime

1 Jean-Paul Sartre, 1969, (607). This passage was first brought to my attention by Lewis Gordon, 1995, (126). My thinking here owes much to Gordon and his use of Sartre.
2 Rudi Bleys, 1995, (44).
3 ibid., (18).
4 Trexler, 1995, (84).
5 Stuart Hall, 1989, (445).
6 Lewis Gordon, 1995 (127).
7 Rudi Bleys, 1993, (192).
8 Jamake Highwater, 1997, (216).
9 ibid., (35).
10 See Baird and Rahim, 2000.

Earth

1 Wilson Duff, 1975 (28).

Wildness

1 Henry David Thoreau, 1968, (226).
2 Henry David Thoreau, 1854, (4).
3 Henry David Thoreau, 1967, (45).
4 Susan Griffin, 1978, (227).
5 The Homomonument is described and quoted in James Saslow, 1999 (288-9).

Dirt

1 Nature Canada Autumn 2001 (27).
2 Hansard September 20, 1994.
3 Bruce Bagemihl, 1999.
4 Bruce Bagemihl, 1999.
5 Catriona Sandilands, 1994.
6 Andrew Lewis, 1998, (3).

7   National Geographic, November 1992.

8   Jacques Cousteau, 1975, (62-5).

9   Catriona Sandilands, op. cit., 23, writes: "A politics that would celebrate 'strangeness' would place queer at the centre, rather than on the margins, of the discursive universe. It is not that we encounter 'the stranger' only when we visit 'the wilderness,' but that s/he/it inhabits even the most everyday of our actions. To treat the world as 'strange' is to open up the possibility of wonder, to speak also with the impenetrable space between the words in our language."

10 Bruce Bagemihl, 1999.

11 Bruce Bagemihl, 1999, explores ways in which acknowledging the widespread existence of animal homosexuality and non-reproductive sexualities invites a radical re-thinking of the natural world.

Money

1   Description based on the research of Gilbert H. Herdt in Papua, New Guinea in the 1970's. Reported in Francis Mondimore, 1996, (16 ff.), and Henning Bech, 1997, (12).

2   John D'Emilio, "Capitalism and Gay Identity," Abelove et.al. (470).

3   I am deeply indebted here and elsewhere in the chapters "Dirt," "Money" and "Family" to Jean-Paul Sartre's *Anti-Semite and Jew*.

Family

1   Alexander Wilson, 1991, points this out.

2   Audre Lorde, 1978 (82).

3   Ranier Maria Rilke, Robert Bly, trans., 1981.

4   See Bruce Bagemihl, 1999, for these and many other examples of animal homosexuality, intersexuality, transgender and non reproductive sexualities.

5   James Hillman, 1996 (85-90).

6   Statistics from U.S. quoted by James Hillman. Statistics Canada, "Mortality: Summary List of Causes," 1997, calculated for ages 10 to 19, based on tables p. (10-13).

7   John D'Emilio, in Abelove et. al., 1993, (475).

Darkness

1   James Baldwin and Nikki Giovanni, A Dialogue, Philadelphia: J. P. Lippincourt, 1973, quoted in Jonathan Katz, 1996, (103).

2   David Roediger, 1994 (13).

3   in David Roediger, 1998, (100).

4   James Baldwin, The Fire Next Time, in 1985, (375). Following quote is also from page 375.

5   Ruth Frankenberg, 1993, (5).

The Mother and The Maid

1   Audre Lorde, 1978, (82).
2   Carl G. Jung and Carl Kerényi, 1949, (179).
3   Carl Jung, 1959, (428).
4   ibid. (123).
5   Catherine Keller asks, "What would it be like if the original continuum from which we all emerge ... [was] neither shattered nor repressed, but extended and transformed?" Quoted by Karin Lofthus Carrington, in Robert H. Hopke, Karen Loftus Carrington and Scott Wirth. (Eds.), 1993, (90). This chapter owes much to Carrington's analysis.

The Tree God

1   Carl Jung and Carl Kerényi, 1949, (98).
2   quoted by Thomas Moore, 1996, (28).
3   Carl Jung and Carl Kerényi, 1949, (93).

Air

1   Plato, Symposium 189C-191D, trans. Will Roscoe, in Will Roscoe, 1995, (156).
2   James Baldwin, 1949, (42).

Laughter

1   William Blake, "The Marriage of Heaven and Hell," 1966, (149).
2   Andrew Hodges and David Hutter, 1974.
3   Carol Pearson, 1991, describes this kind of trust as an aspect of the Fool.
4   Madeline McMurray, (45).
5   Ralph Maud, ed., 1978, (124 ff.).
6   Randy P. Conner et. al., 1997, (114).
7   Don Handleman.
8   Carl Jung, 1971, (147).
9   In December 1999 the CBS News program "60 Minutes" broadcast a segment highlighting the pervasive anti-gay bigotry in the United States military.

Innocence

1   Mark Thompson, 1987, (xvi).
2   Mark Thompson, ed., 1991, (xviii).

Effeminacy

1   Richard Trexler, 1995, (30); see also (23-31).
2   Leo Bersani, "Is the Rectum a Grave?" in Douglas Crimp, ed., 1988, (197-222).

3   As, for example, in ancient Sparta or Japanese samurai traditions.
4   Michel Foucault, 1978, (43).
5   Luce Irigaray, "When the Goods Get Together," in Elaine Marks and Isabella de Courtivron, eds., (107), emphasis original.
6   Will Roscoe, 1995, (261).
7   Sigmund Freud, "Civilization and its Discontents," 1930, in James Strachey, ed., 1985, Vol. 12, (289n); (304).
8   Sigmund Freud, "Splitting of the Ego in the Process of defense," 1940, in James Strachey, ed., Vol. 11., (462).
9   Frank Browning, 1994, (87, 89).
10 Klaus Theweleit, Male Fantasies, trans Chris Turner and Erica Carter, Cambridge: polity Press, 1989, Volume 2 p 138, quoted by Murray Healy, 1996.
11 see Scott Wirth, in Hopke et. al. (eds.), 1993 (201) for a telling list of the effeminacies by which gay men come to "give themselves away," even while they try not to acknowledge their homosexuality.
12 Wayne Wooden and Jay Parker, 1982.

Annunciation

1   Henry David Thoreau, 1841 Journal, quoted in Katz, 1976, (210).
2   Eve Kosofky Sedgwick, 1990, (68).
3   Thomas Moore, 1996, (104).
4   Stephen Riggins interview 1983.
5   As Henning Bech, 1997, points out. He writes: "At the same time a surface is formed, an inner, a depth, an essence develops – a self. This is partly a kind of residuum of what was before and what otherwise is and cannot get absorbed in the surface: being Fred Bloggs, siring his children, boozing away his pay, and so on. . . . What we have, then, is a person who has fallen into two parts: an inner self on the one hand, and a surface on the other." (164-5).
6   Dag Hammarskjöld, 1964, (62).
7   Dag Hammarskjöld, 1964, (83).
8   ibid., (127). The quote in the following paragraph is also from page 127.

Sky God

1   Sander Gilman describes Ham as guilty of the "most heinous of all sexual acts, the same-sex gaze." In fact the "most heinous" act is surely not the gaze itself, but the father-son incest which is implied. See S.L. Gilman, 1989, Sexuality.
2   James Baldwin, 1949, (42).
3   Colin Spence, 1995, (56).
6   Luce Irigaray, "When the Goods Get Together," in Elaine Marks and Isabella de Courtivron, eds., (107), emphasis original.
5   James Baldwin, 1985, (234); see also 1949.
6   Peter London, 1989, (80) discusses not knowing as a key to creativity.

Suffering

1   "The Worst of It," in Essex Hemphill, ed., 1991 (143).
2   see James Brooke, 1998.
3   Joannes Malalas, Chronographia, quoted in Boswell, 1980, (172).
4   James Baldwin, 1985, (376).
5   This idea is more fully explored in my paper "Sexual Subject / Sexual Object," Resources for Feminist Research," Volume 19, No. 3 & 4, 1992.
6   Rollo May, 1969, (30-31).
7   James Baldwin develops this idea in his early (1949) essay, "The Preservation of Innocence," linking impoverished gender roles with homophobia.

Rage

1   Valerie Solanas wrote and self-published the **SCUM** Manifesto in 1967. It was reprinted in 1996 by **AK** Press, San Francisco and Edinburgh.
2   quoted in Frank Browning, 1994.
3   ibid.
4   see Aeschylus (525-456 **BC**), The Eumenides.

Sex

1   "The Dangerous Painters," quoted in Saslow, 1999 (250).
2   see godhatesfags.com, emphasis original.
3   Joseph Campbell et. al., 1991, (7).

Pedophilia

1   Carole Jenny et. al., 1994.
2   Patterson, C. J. "Children of lesbian and gay parents." Child Development 1992; 63:1025-42.18.
3   A. Nicolas Groth and H. Jean Birnbaum, 1978, "Adult Sexual Orientation and Attraction to underage persons," Archives of Sexual Behavior, 7 (3), (175-181).
4   Canadian Adoption Attitudes Survey, 2002, by Charlene Miall, McMaster University and Karen March, Carleton University; General Social Survey, 1999, by the National Opinion Research Centre, University of Chicago.
5   Will Roscoe, 1995, (232).
6   John Boswell, 1980, (250-251).
7   Children's sexual play and experimentation is happily accepted in other cultures (See C. S. Ford and F. A. Beach, 1951). Even here, where child sexuality is not supposed to happen, Alfred Kinsey reports 57% of adults he interviewed admitted engaging in some form of pre-adolescent sex play. In most recent representations of children, their interest in sex is denied, punished, and taken as proof of abuse. Typically, a parents' guide to harassment and abuse in sports cautions that "sexualized behavior in children is the result of sexual abuse." (What Parents Can Do About Harassment and Abuse in Sport, compiled by Marg

McGregor, Executive Director, Canadian Association for Women and Sport and Physical Activity, available on the internet.) But to say that children can be sexual is not to say that pedophilia is tolerable. See, on the following page, that I believe adult-child sexual contact is always exploitative in a society where children are silenced and deprived of choice.

8   Shere Hite, 1994.

9   The title of an article in The Body Politic, a Toronto magazine, which led to police raids on the publication, 1980.

10 A Supreme Court decision in the Robin Sharpe case allowed his writing, though he was sentenced for possession of photographs (taken by himself) of children engaged in sex with one another and with adults. Sharpe's acquittal on the grounds of artistic merit provoked wide public outrage, leading the federal government to consider new legislation removing the artistic merit defense in child pornography cases.

11 Adrienne Rich, "Compulsory Heterosexuality and Lesbian Existence," 1986, (53).

12 Audre Lorde, "Uses of the Erotic: The Erotic as Power," 1984, (56).

13 As Marjorie Garber points out, 1992.

14 Luce Irigaray, in Elaine Marks and Isabelle de Courtivron, Eds., 1980, (110).

15 Adrienne Rich, 1986, (54).

16 Audre Lorde, 1978, (59).

17 Firestone, 1970, (96).

Danger

1   Confessions 3. 1, quoted by Boswell, 1980, (135).

2   John Ayto, 1990 (48).

3   quoted in Nealy, 1995, (Sept. 1).

4   Wittig, 1992 (45).

5   See Halperin, 1995, (73-77).

6   Eric Clarke, Virtuous Vice: Homoeroticism and the Public Sphere, (Durham: Duke University Press, 2000), quoted by Lisbeth Lipari, 2002, (170).

7   Thomas Merton, 1956, writes: "True poverty is that of the beggar who is glad to receive alms from anyone, but especially from God. False poverty is that of a man who pretends to have the self-sufficiency of an angel. True poverty, then, is a receiving and giving of thanks." (94).

Another Country

1   (sic). Nicole Brossard, "Green Night of Labyrinth Park," trans. Lou Nelson, in Betsy Warland, ed., 1991, (197).

2   Lady Eleanor Butler and Sarah Ponsonby set up house together in Wales in 1778. They lived together in Llangollen for fifty years, hosting many distinguished guests and becoming famous in England for their independent life, their manly attire, and their devotion to one another.

3   ibid., (197).

4   Walt Whitman, 1860, Bowers, ed., (114)

5   Aaron Betsky, 1997, (59).

NOTES

Environments

1 Robert Duncan, 1964, (62).
2 Gordon Brent Ingram, "Marginality and the Landscapes of Erotic Alien(n)ations," in Gordon Brent Ingram, Anne-Marie Bouthillette and Yolanda Retter., eds., 1997.
3 Alexander Wilson, 1991, (17).
4 Alexander Wilson, 1991, (13).
5 Walt Whitman, Enfans d'Adam, Bowers, ed. (61).
6 Monique Wittig, 1992.
7 Ralph Maud, 1982.
8 Bruce Bagemihl, Biological Exuberance: Animal Homosexuality and Natural Diversity, New York: St. Martin's Press, 1999.

Absence

1 Henning Bech, 1997, (62). Emphasis original.
2 Alan Bray, 1990.
3 Karin Lofthus Carrington in Hopke et. al., 1993.
4 The Letters of Emily Dickinson, eds. Thomas H. Johnson and Theodora Wars (Cambridge: Harvard University Press, 1958), Letter 96, quoted in Lillian Faderman, 1981, (176).
5 Margot Francis, 1996, (36-7).
6 Edward O. Lauman, John H. Gagnon, Robert T. Michael and Stuart Michaels, The Social Organization of Sexuality: Sexual Practices in the United States (Chicago: University of Chicago Press, 1994), reported in Francis Mark Mondimore, 1996, (89).
7 Sigmund Freud, Standard Edition Vol.7, (145-146 n.).
8 Henning Bech, op.cit., (55).
9 ibid., (82).
10 quoted by David Halperin, 1995, (77-78).

The Body

1 Judith Butler, in Diana Fuss, ed., (21), emphasis original.
2 Joan Nestle, 1992, (14).
3 Joan Nestle, 1992, (14).
4 This paragraph in particular and this chapter in general owe much to Sue Ellen Case, "Toward a Butch-Femme Aesthetic," in Abelove et. al. (1993), p. 294- 306.
5 Jan Brown in Joan Nestle, ibid., (414).
6 Judith Butler in Liz Kotz, 1992, (85).
7 Barbara Duden, 1993.
8 Herbert Marcuse, 1960.

Placemaking

1 Judy Grahn, 1984, (83).
2 Christopher Alexander et. al., 1977, (299).

3   Christopher Alexander et. al., 1977, (353).
4   Sandra Butler and Barbara Rosenblum, 1996, Spinsters Ink.
5   Jim Fouratt, 1999.
6   Elsie Jay, "Domestic Dykes: The Politics of 'In-difference,'" in Gordon Brent Ingram et. al, eds, (165).
7   Aaron Betsky, 1997, (193).
8   Christopher Alexander et. al., op. cit.

Limits

1   Jean Cocteau, 1928.
2   James Broughton in Mark Thompson, 1987, (205), says "It is essential that gay politics keep eroding homophobia, but the most exciting task that remains is how we can persuade the homophobes what a great gay life all men could be romping in."
3   In this paragraph, I am drawing on the work of M. Scott Peck, 1997. Stereotypes, Archetypes and Activism
1   Canadian Press / Leger Marketing Executive Report June 22, 2001
2   Christopher Banks, 2003.
3   Byrne Fone, 2000 (418-419). See also National Gay and Lesbian Task Force Policy Institute Anti-Gay/Lesbian Violence, Victimization and Defamation at ngltf.com and a Canadian study by the 519 Community Centre in Toronto for the Department of Justice looking at the issue of violence in the LGBT community.
4   December 20, 2002.
5   Gay and Lesbian Educators of B.C., 2000, Background Report (27).
6   A recent article in the Globe and Mail on a B.C. Supreme Court decision endorsing the right of gay and lesbian couples to marry says that "redefining marriage would amount to a massive human experiment" and admit a terrifying disorder to social relationships. Katherine Young and Paul Nathanson, "Keep it all in the family," Globe and Mail, May 2, 2003. (A15).
7   Sean Cahill, Ph.D. and Kenneth T. Jones; C. Jenney et. al., 1994.
8   Stephen O. Murray and Will Roscoe, 1998.
9   Will Roscoe, 1995 (210-215).
10 Pat Robertson from Didi Herman, 1997. Falwell quote is on the internet.
11 Edward Carpenter, The Intermediate Sex, from Selected Writings, ed. N. Grieg, London, 1984, quoted in Rudi Bleys, 1995, (244).
12 Mark Thompson, 1987 (187).
13 Ibid. (187).
14 Joseph Campbell in conversation with Michael Toms, 1988, (23-24).
15 bell hooks, 2001, (76-77).
16 Gary Kinsman, 2003.

Bibliography

Abelove, Henry, Michèle Aina Barale and David Halperin. (Eds). (1993) The Lesbian and Gay Studies Reader. New York and London: Routledge

Alexander, Christopher, Sara Ishikawa, and Murray Silverstein with Max Jacobson, Ingrid Fiksdahl-King and Shlomo Angel. (1977). A Pattern Language: Towns, Buildings, Construction. New York: Oxford University Press.

Ayto, John. (1990). Dictionary of Word Origins. London: Bloomsbury.

Bagemihl, Bruce. (1999). Biological Exuberance: Animal Homosexuality and Natural Diversity. New York: St. Martin's Press.

Baird, Vanessa and Shuaib Rahim. (Eds.). (2000) "Out South: Sexual Minorities in the Majority World." New Internationalist, October 2000.

Baldwin, James. (1985). The Price of the Ticket: Collected Nonfiction 1948-1985. New York: St. Martin's / Marek

_____. (1949). "The Preservation of Innocence." Zero, Summer 1949, Volume 1, No. 2, Tangiers, Morocco. Reprinted Fall 1989 in Outlook, Volume 2, No. 2, San Francisco.

Banks, Christopher, Rochon Associated Human Resource Management Consulting Inc., The Cost of Homophobia: Literature Review on the Human Impact of Homophobia in Canada, Gay and Lesbian Health Services, Saskatoon, Saskatchewan, May 2003.

Bech, Henning. (1997). When Men Meet: Homosexuality and Modernity. trans. T. Mesquit and Tim Davies. originally published in Denmark, 1986. Chicago: University of Chicago Press.

Benjamin, Jessica. (1983). "Master and Slave: The Fantasy of Erotic Domination." in Ann Snitow, Christine Stansell and Sharon Thompson, (Eds.). Powers of Desire: The Politics of Sexuality. New York: Monthly Review Press.

Betsky, Aaron. (1997). Queer Space: Architecture and Same-Sex Desire. New York: William Morrow and Company.

Blake, William. (1966). Complete Writings. Oxford: Oxford University Press.

Bleys, Rudi C. (1995). The Geography of Perversion: Male-to-Male Sexual Behavior Outside the West and the Ethnographic Imagination, 1750-1918. New York: New York University Press.

Boswell, John. (1980). Christianity, Social Tolerance and Homosexuality: Gay People in Western Europe from the Beginning of the Christian Era to the 14th Century. Chicago and London: University of Chicago Press, 1980.

Bray, Alan. "Homosexuality and the sign of male friendship in Elizabethan England." History Workshop 1990, 1-19.

Brooke, James. (1998). "Witnesses trace brutal killing of gay student." New York Times, November 21st.

Browning, Frank. (1994). The Culture of Desire: Paradox and Perversity in Gay Lives Today. New York: Vintage Books (Random House).

Byrne, Robert (ed.). 1,911 Best Things Anybody Ever Said.

Cahill, Sean, Ph.D. and Kenneth T. Jones, "Child Sexual Abuse and Homosexuality: The Long History of the "Gays as Pedophiles" Fallacy," National Gay and Lesbian Task Force paper, available online at ngltf.com.

Campbell, Joseph, (1988) with Bill Moyers. Betty Sue Flowers, ed. The Power of Myth, New York: Doubleday.

Campbell, Joseph in conversation with Michael Toms. (1988). An Open Life. New York: Larson Publications.

Canadian Press / Leger Marketing Executive Report June 22, 2001, Canadian Perceptions of Homosexuality.

Cirlot, J.E. (1971). A Dictionary of Symbols. Trans. Jack Sage. New York: Dover, 2002.

Cocteau, Jean. (1928). The White Book. trans. Margaret Crosland. San Francisco: City Lights, 1989.

Colum, Padraic. (1930) Myths of the World. New York: Grosset & Dunlap.

Conner, Randy P. (1991). Blossom of Bone: Reclaiming Connections Between Homoeroticism and the Sacred. San Francisco: HarperSanFrancisco.

Conner, Randy P., David Hatfield Sparks and Mariya Sparks. (1997). Cassell's Encyclopedia of Queer Myth, Symbol and Spirit. London: Cassell.

Cousteau, Jaques. (1975). The Ocean World of Jaques Cousteau. Volume 2. Toronto: Prentice-Hall.

Crimp, Douglas (Ed.). (1988). AIDS: Cultural Analysis, Cultural Activism. London and Cambridge: MIT Press.

Deming, Barbara. Ed. Jane Meyerding. (1984). We are All Part of One Another: A Barbara Deming Reader. Philadelphia: New Society Publishers.

Downing, Christine. (1989). Myths and Mysteries of Same-Sex Love. New York: Continuum.

Duden, Barbara. (1993) Disembodying Women: Perspectives on Pregnancy and the Unborn. London and Cambridge: Harvard University Press.

Duff, Wilson. (1975) Images Stone B.C.: Thirty Centuries of Northwest Coast Indian Sculpture. Saanichton: Hancock House Publishers.

Duncan, Robert. (1964). Roots and Branches: Poems by Robert Duncan. New York: Charles Scribner.

Ellmann, Richard. (1987) Oscar Wilde Markham, Ontario: Viking / Penguin.

Estes, Clarissa Pinkola. (1992). Women Who Run With the Wolves: Myths and Stories of the Wild Woman Archetype. New York: Ballantine Books.

Faderman, Lillian. (1981). Surpassing the Love of Men: Romantic Friendship and Love Between Women from the Renaissance to the Present. New York: Quality Paperback Book Club, 1994.

Firestone, Shulamith. (1970, 1971). The Dialectic of Sex: A Case for Feminist Revolution. New York: Bantam Books.

Foucault, Michel. (1978). The History of Sexuality. Volume I. trans. Robert Hurley. New York: Pantheon.

Ford, C.S. and Beach, F.A. (1951). Patterns

of Sexual Behavior. New York: Harper and Row.

Fone, Byrne. (2000) Homophobia: A History. New York: Picador

Fouratt, Jim. (1999). "The question remains: what do we want?" The Many Faces of Pride: **LGNY** Special Pride Issue, June 23, 1999, New York City, republished in an e-mail discussion, "Bring Equality Out of the Closet," August 1999.

Francis, Margot. ""For this girl was my grand passion ... Re-interpreting the first large-scale survey of women's sexuality in America (1929)." Lesbians and Politics issue, Canadian Women's Studies cws/cf. North York, York University, Vol. 16. No. 2. May 1996.

Frankenberg, Ruth. (1993). White Women, Race Matters: The Social Construction of Whiteness. Minneapolis: University of Minnesota Press.

Freud, Sigmund. On Metapsychology and the Theory of Psychoanalysis. The Pelican Freud Library. Ed., trans. James Strachey. Vol. 11. Middlesex, England: Penguin, 1985.

_____. Civilization, Society and Religion. Vol. 12.

_____. (1953-1974) The Standard Edition of the Complete Psychological Works of Sigmund Freud, Ed., trans. James Strachey. Vol. 7. London: Hogarth Press.

Fuss, Diana, ed. (1991) Inside / Out: Lesbian Theories; Gay Theories. New York and London: Routledge.

Gay and Lesbian Educators of B.C.. (2000) Challenging Homophobia in Schools.

Garber, Marjorie B. (1992). Vested Interests: Cross-Dressing and Cultural Anxiety. New York: Routledge.

Gordon, Lewis R. (1995). Bad Faith and Antiblack Racism. New Jersey: Humanities Press.

Grahn, Judy. (1984). Another Mother Tongue: Gay Words; Gay Worlds. Boston: Beacon Press.

Griffin, Susan. (1978) Woman and Nature: The Roaring Inside Her. New York and San Francisco: Harper and Row.

Halperin, David M. (1995). Saint Foucault: Towards a Gay Hagiography. New York / Oxford: Oxford University Press.

Hall, Stuart. (1989) "New ethnicities." David Morley and Kuan-Hsing Chen, eds. (1996). Stuart Hall: Critical Dialogues in Cultural Studies. London and New York: Routledge.

Hall, Stuart and Paul du Gay. (1996) Questions of Cultural Identity. London, Thousand Oaks, New Delhi: Sage.

Hammarskjöld, Dag. (1964) Markings. trans. Leif Sjöberg and W. H. Auden. London: Faber and Faber.

Handelman, Don: "The Ritual-Clown: Attributes and Affinities." Reprinted on the masks.org website by permission from Anthropos, 76.1981: 321—370.

Healy, Murray. (1996). Gay Skins: Class, Masculinity and Queer Appropriation. Cassell: London.

Hemphill, Essex (Ed.). (1991). Brother to Brother: New Writings by Black Gay Men. Boston: Alyson Publications.

Herman, Didi. "The Gay Agenda is the Devil's Agenda: The Christian Right's Vision and the Role of the State." essay published in part in L. Eyre and L. Roman, eds. Dangerous Territories: The Backlash in Education (New York: Routeledge, 1997) and on the internet.

Highwater, Jamake. (1997). The Mythology of Transgression: Homosexuality as Metaphor. New York and Oxford: Oxford

University Press.

Hillman, James. (1996) The Soul's Code. New York: Random House.

Hite, Shere. (1994). The Hite Report on the Family: Growing Up Under Patriarchy. New York: Grove Press.

Hoagland, Sarah Lucia. (1988). Lesbian Ethics: Toward New Value. Palo Alto: Institute of Lesbian Studies.

Hodges, Andrew and David Hutter. (1974). With Downcast Gays. Gay liberation pamphlet republished on the web, 1997 at www.wadham.ox.ac.uk/~ahodges/wdg/

hooks, bell. (2001). Salvation: Black People and Love. New York: HarperCollins.

Hopke, Robert H. (1989). Jung, Jungians and Homosexuality. Boston: Shambhala Publications.

Hopke, Robert H., Karen Loftus Carrington and Scott Wirth. (Eds.) (1993) Same-Sex Love As a Path to Wholeness. Boston and London: Shambhala.

Ingram, Gordon Brent, Anne-Marie Douthillette and Yolanda Retter. (Eds.). (1997). Queers in Space: Communities, Public Places, Sites of Resistance. Seattle: Bay Press.

Jackson, Graham. (1993). The Living Room Mysteries: Patterns of Male Intimacy Book II. Toronto: Inner City Books.

_____. The Secret Lore of Gardening: Patterns of Male Intimacy. Toronto: Inner City Books.

Jagose, Annamarie. (1996). Queer Theory: An Introduction. New York: New York University Press.

Jenny, Carole, Thomas Roesler and Kimberly Payer, "Are Children at Risk for Sexual Abuse by Homosexuals?" Pediatrics 94 no. I (1994): 41-44.

Jung, Carl G. and Carl Kerényi. (1949).

Essays on a Science of Mythology: The Myth of the Divine Child and the Mysteries of Eleusis. trans. R.F.C. Hull. Bollingen Series XXII. Princeton: Princeton University Press.

Jung, Carl G. (1959). (1993). ed. Violet Staub de Laszlo. The Basic Writings of C. G. Jung. New York: Modern Library.

_____. (1971). Four Archetypes. (From Vol. 9 Collected Works). Edited by Gerhard Adler. Translated by R.F.C. Hull. Princeton: Princeton University Press.

Katz, Jonathan Ned. (1976) Gay American History: Lesbians and Gay Men in the USA New York: Thomas and Crowell.

_____. (1995, 1996) The Invention of Heterosexuality. New York: Plume / Penguin.

Kincaid, James R. (1998) Erotic Innocence: The Culture of Child Molesting. Duke University Press.

Kinsman, Gary. "Class, History and the Future of Queer Movements," workshop presented at Rainbow Visions, EGALE Canada Conference, Montreal, May 16-19, 2003.

Knapp, Gottfried. (1999). Angels, Archangels, and all the Company of Heaven. New York: Prestel.

Knudtson, Peter and David Suzuki. (1992). Wisdom of the Elders. Toronto: Stoddart.

Kritzman, Lawrence. (Ed.) (1988) Politics, Philosophy and Culture: Interviews and Other Writings of Michel Foucault, 1977-84. London: Routledge Champman Hall.

Kotz, Liz. (1992). "The Body You Want: Liz Kotz Interviews Judith Butler." Artforum, Vol. 31, No. 3, November 1992.

Lacan, Jaques. (1977). Écrits: A Selection. trans. Alan Sheridan. New York: W.W.

Norton.

Levay, Simon. (1996). Queer Science: The Use and Abuse of Research in Homosexuality. Cambridge: MIT Press.

Lewis, Andrew. (1998). "Restoration Ecology Assists the Land to Heal Itself," The Acorn: Newsletter of the Saltspring Island Conservancy, No. 6, June 1998.

Lipari, Lisbeth. (2002). "Queering the Public Sphere: Liberalism and the Rhetoric of Rights," Argumentation and Advocacy 38: 169-175.

London, Peter. (1986). No More Secondhand Art: Awakening the Artist Within. Boston: Shambhala.

Lorde, Audre. (1978). The Black Unicorn. New York: W. W. Norton.

_____. (1984). Sister Outsider: Essays and Speeches. Freedom, CA: The Crossing Press.

Lucie-Smith, Edward. (1997). Ars Erotica: An Arousing History of Erotic Art. New York: Rizzoli.

McMurray, Madeline. Illuminations: The Healing Image.

Marks, Elaine and Isabelle de Courtivron. (Eds.). (1980). New French Feminisms. Amherst: University of Massachusetts Press.

Marcuse, Herbert. (1960). Reason and Revolution. Boston: Beacon Press.

Masson, Jeffrey. When Elephants Weep: The Emotional Lives of Animals. (1995). New York: Delacorte Press.

Maud, Ralph, ed. (1978). The Salish People: The Local Contribution of Charles Hill-Tout. Volume III: The Mainland Halkomelem. Vancouver: Talon Books.

_____. (1982). A Guide to B.C. Indian Myth and Legend. Vancouver: Talon Books.

May, Rollo. (1969). Love and Will. New York: W.W. Norton.

_____. (1991). The Cry For Myth. New York: W.W.Norton.

Merton, Thomas. (1956). Thoughts in Solitude. New York: Farrar, Straus and Giroux.

Miles, Chistopher with John Julius Norwich. (1997). Love in the Ancient World. London: Seven Dials.

Mondimore, Francis Mark. (1996). A Natural History of Homosexuality. Baltimore and London: The Johns Hopkins University Press.

Monette, Paul. (1992). Becoming A Man: Half a Life Story. New York: HarperCollins.

Moon, Beverly, ed. (1991). An Encyclopedia of Archetypal Symbolism. Boston and London: Shambala.

Moore, Thomas. (1992). Care of the Soul: A Guide for Cultivating Depth and Sacredness in Everyday Life. New York: HarperCollins.

_____. (1994). Soul Mates: Honoring the Mysteries of Love & Relationship. Toronto: HarperCollins Canada.

_____. (1996). The Re-Enchantment of Everyday Life. New York: HarperCollins.

Murray, Stephen O. Will Roscoe. (1998). Boy Wives and Female Husbands: Studies of African Homosexualities. New York: Palgrave, 1998.

Nealy, Eleanor. (1995). Amazon Spirit: Daily Meditations for Lesbians in Recovery. New York: Perigreen.

Nestle, Joan (Ed.). (1992). The Persistent Desire: A Femme-Butch Reader. Boston: Alyson Publications.

Ott, Christopher. (1999). "Bring equality out of the closet." Los Angeles Times,

ORIENTATION

June 22, 1999. republished in an e-mail discussion, August 1999.

Pearson, Carol. (1991). Awakening the Heroes Within. San Francisco: HarperSanFrancisco.

Peck, M. Scott. (1997) People of the Lie: The Hope for Healing Human Evil. 2nd Edition. New York: Simon and Schuster.

Rawson, Philip, ed. (1973) Primitive Erotic Art. New York: G.P. Putnam's Sons.

Rich, Adrienne. (1986) Blood, Bread, and Poetry: Selected Prose 1979-1985. New York: W.W. Norton.

Rilke, Ranier Maria. (1981) trans. Robert Bly. Selected Poems of Ranier Maria Rilke. New York: Harper and Row

Roediger, David. (1994). Towards the Abolition of Whiteness. New York: Verso.

_____, (Ed.). (1998). Black on White: Black Writers on What it Means to be White. New York: Schocken Books.

Roscoe, Will. (1998). Changing Ones: Third and Fourth Genders in Native North America. New York: St. Martin's Press.

_____. (1995). Queer Spirits: A Gay Men's Myth Book. Boston: Beacon Press.

Sandars, N. K., trans. (1960). The Epic of Gilgamesh. Penguin.

Sandilands, Catriona. "Lavender's Green? Some Thoughts on Queer(y)ing Environmental Politics." "Queer Nature," special issue of UnderCurrents, York University Faculty of Environmental Studies, May 1994.

Sandfort, Theo, Edward Brongessma and Alex VanNaersen, eds. (1991). Male Intergenerational Intimacy: Historical, Sociocultural and Legal Perspectives. New York and London: Haworth Press.

Sartre, Jean-Paul. (1948, 1995) Anti-Semite and Jew: An Exploration of the Etiol-

ogy of Hate. trans. George J. Becker. New York: Schocken Books.

_____. (1969). Being and Nothingness: An Essay on Phenomenological Ontology. trans. Hazel E. Barnes. London: Methuen and Co. Ltd.

Saslow, James M. (1999). Pictures and Passions: A History of Homosexuality in the Visual Arts. New York: Viking

Schmidgall, Gary. (1998). Walt Whitman: A Gay Life. New York: Plume / Penguin.

Sedgwick, Eve Kosofky. (1990). Epistemology of the Closet. Berkeley and Los Angeles: University of California Press.

Spence, Colin. (1995). Homosexuality in History. New York: Harcourt, Brace and Company.

Synder, Gary. (1992). "Coming in to the Watershed." speech given at a conference for the Centre for California Studies, February 6, 1992. Printed in Scott Walker (Ed.). (1993). The Graywolf Annual Ten: Changing Community. Saint Paul: Graywolf Press.

Stewart, Hilary (1977) Indian Fishing: Early Methods on the Northwest Coast. Vancouver, J.J. Douglas Ltd.

Thomas, Keith. (1984) Man and the Natural World: A History of the Modern Sensibility. New York: Pantheon.

Thompson, Mark. (1984). The Long Road to Freedom: The Advocate History of the Gay and Lesbian Movement. New York: St. Martin's Press.

_____. (1987). Gay Spirit: Myth and Meaning. New York: St. Martin's Press.

_____, ed. (1991)Leatherfolk: Radical Sex, People, Politics and Practice Boston: Alyson.

_____. (1994). Gay Soul: Finding the Heart of Gay Spirit in Nature. San Fran-

188

cisco: HarperSanFrancisco.

Thoreau, Henry David. (1968) "Walking, or the Wild," in The Writings of Henry David Thoreau, Vol. 15, New York: AMS Press.

_____. (1854). (1995). Walden: or, Life in the Woods. New York: Dover Publications, Inc.

_____. Bode, Carl. (Ed.) (1967). The Selected Journals of Henry David Thoreau. New York: New American Library.

Trexler, Richard C. (1995). Sex and Conquest: Gendered Violence, Political Order, and the European Conquest of the Americas. Ithaca, New York: Cornell University Press.

Trinh T. Minh-ha. (1989). Woman, Native, Other: Writing Postcoloniality and Feminism. Bloomington and Indianapolis: Indiana University Press.

Warland, Betsy. (Ed.). (1991) InVersions: Writing by Dykes, Queers and Lesbians. Vancouver: Press Gang Publishers.

Warren, Carol A. B. (1974). Identity and Community in the Gay World. New York / Toronto: John Wiley and Sons.

Whitman, Walt. Fredson Bowers, Ed. (1955). Whitman's Manuscripts: Leaves of Grass (1860), A Parallel Text. Chicago and London: University of Chicago Press.

Wilson, Alexander. (1991) The Culture of Nature: North American Landscape from Disney to the Exxon Valdez. Toronto: Between the Lines.

Wittig, Monique. (1992). The Straight Mind and Other Essays. Boston: Beacon Press.

Wooden, Wayne and Jay Parker. (1982). Men Behind Bars: Sexual Exploitation in Prison. New York: Da Capo.

Photo: Billie Woods

About the Author

Caffyn Jesse works as a Somatic Sex Educator. She teaches workshops and classes to people from around the world at her Salt Spring Island studio and online. A recent book, published in 2015, is *Erotic Massage for Healing and Pleasure*. Jesse teaches the Certified Somatic Sex Educator and Certified Sexological Bodyworker trainings in Canada. She offers online programs through her website at www.erospirit.ca.

Jesse moved to Salt Spring Island with her partner, Mearnie Summers, in 1996. Soon after, she began to work towards the founding of a non-profit society that could represent the voices and needs of queer people on the island, in the midst of the vitriolic "gay marriage" debates in Canada. She coordinated a health research project for GLOSSI (Gays and Lesbians of Salt Spring Island) that resulted in the publication *Gay and Lesbian Health on Salt Spring Island: A Resource for Health Care Providers*. She served on the board of GLOSSI for 15 years. She was involved in organizing the island's first Pride celebrations.

Before moving to Salt Spring Island, Jesse was editor and publisher at *Gallerie*, a quarterly publication on women in the arts. She challenged the art world to integrate lesbian difference, and challenged lesbian artists to speak of how their sexual orientation informed their work. Between 1990-2005 she developed her own artwork and writing exploring queer difference, offered workshops, and published a widely-acclaimed website on "Mapping Queer Meanings" (www.queermap.com).

119

Made in the USA
San Bernardino, CA
12 December 2016